The memorizing of Scripture is more than a discipline; it's an act of faith by which we testify to our belief in the life-changing power of God's Word and its inspiration of the Holy Spirit. Despite agreeing with the sentiment, few of us take the time to regularly dwell on the Bible, much less hide it in our hearts, and that's precisely why *The Psalm 119 Experience* is so needed. In this book, John has not only laid out for us the challenge of memorizing the longest chapter in Scripture, but also given us the plan to complete it. *The Psalm 119 Experience* is the means by which you and I, like John, might hide God's Word in our hearts that we might not sin against Him (Ps. 119:10). This book will not only help you memorize the Bible; it will lift your heart and soul to experience the God behind it. So if you don't have time, now is the time. The God of the Bible is waiting.

Michael Kelley, author of *Boring* and
Wednesdays Were Pretty Normal, director of discipleship
at LifeWay Christian Resources

John Kramp has rightly called his devotional guide *The Psalm 119 Experience*, for in the Scripture we encounter God. As the Spirit of God applies the word of God to our minds, we come to know God and to taste his goodness; we are comforted, convicted, and corrected; we are liberated from false notions and harmful behaviors. These are the experiences that John aims to make ours by setting before us the fruit of his meditation on Psalm 119. He has hit his mark. John's insight into both the word of God and the human soul are deep and accurate. He applies the message of this psalm to the realities of life leading us to an encounter with God that is not found in a quick and surface reading. Let him be your guide.

Scott Patty, pastor of Grace Community Church in
Nashville, Tennessee

I've always loved Psalm 119, and after experiencing this devotional journey, I now better understand why I love it so much.

Each verse is not only about God's Word, but it's about life—the ups and downs, the highs and lows, and the God who is present in it all. John Kramp creatively turns a long, and sometimes intimidating, psalm about the Word of God into an accessible daily walk with God. Step by step, this devotional journey will draw you to delight in and live by God's Word.

Jennifer Rothschild, author of *Lessons I Learned in the Dark, Self Talk, Soul Talk,* and *God Is Just Not Fair: Finding Hope When Life Doesn't Make Sense,* founder of Fresh Grounded Faith events and womensministry.net

The Psalm 119 Experience offers concise, spiritual concepts, profound yet easily understood. Seldom have I felt the force of passion in a creative project as I did in John Kramp's desire to bring Psalm 119 to a transformational understanding for believers in Jesus Christ. This has been a long and patient journey. Through perseverance and God's increase, a clear and glorious presentation of Psalm 119 has come into full bloom.

Greg Nelson, writer and producer

THE
PSALM
119
EXPERIENCE

A DEVOTIONAL JOURNEY
YOU WILL NOT FORGET

JOHN KRAMP

B&H
PUBLISHING GROUP
NASHVILLE, TENNESSEE

978-0-8054-6673-7

Published by B&H Publishing Group
Nashville, Tennessee

Dewey Decimal Classification: 242.5
Subject Heading: DEVOTIONAL LITERATURE \
CHRISTIAN LIFE \ BIBLE. O.T. PSALM 119

All song lyrics are written by the author using the specific
text from the Holman Christian Standard Bible (HCSB).

1 2 3 4 5 6 7 8 • 18 17 16 15 14

Selah Grace Gibson and Elijah Wesley Baker

May the God of grace give you hearts
for His Word throughout your lives.

Acknowledgments

Before I began writing books, I read "acknowledgment" pages others wrote and thought, *Isn't that nice.* Now I know such pages have nothing to do with being "nice." For me, a book without an "acknowledgment" page is scandalous, like a father failing to mention the role his wife played in giving birth to their child.

No book screams for an "acknowledgment" page like this one. I wrote this book and the songs that support it only for myself. Others saw the potential for my Psalm 119 experience to help others experience God in a fresh way through this incredible chapter of the Bible.

Lynn Marie, my wife and all-time best friend, waited patiently for more than a year while I sang songs in the shower, scribbled out songs in my study, and began putting lyrics to music. Then when I told her I wanted to have Nashville studio musicians record these 22 songs (a very expensive proposition, I discovered, for which we paid for personally), she supported me at each step along the way. Lynn Marie, thank you for allowing me to do this project rather than remodeling the bathroom as we had planned.

Greg Nelson, my heart-friend and veteran songwriter and producer, listened to my first twelve songs as I sung them and played the guitar (a painful experience for anyone) and didn't laugh. In fact, he said I must write all two 22 songs and when I did, he would help me get them produced and recorded. I could have never afforded Greg's expertise but he gave it joyfully.

Through Greg, others joined the creative team: Dennis Allen, an accomplished songwriter and producer in his own rite, led me through the maze in which I constantly got lost and then worked with Greg to get the project produced. Steve Dady did engineering magic in his studio and worked with Greg and Dennis to line up some of Nashville's finest session players—Dave Cleveland, Craig Nelson, Jason Webb, Eric Darken, Melodie Kirkpatrick, Kim Flemming, Vicky Hampton, Shane McDonnell, Terry White, and Kirk Kirkland. Watching these gifted musicians take my feeble musical efforts and bring them to life gave me days of memories in the studio I'll always cherish. By the way, if you get the chance to listen to the 22 songs that go with this project, know that any limitations in the songs come from me; the beauty in these songs come from these people exercising their musical gifts.

I want to thank the people in LifeWay Church Resources who I had the privilege to lead for many years. They were the first to hear some of the song in their raw form in a chapel service I will never forget. Thank you, friends, for the great gift you gave me that day.

Devin Maddox at B&H Publishing Group championed this devotional book and went out on a limb to help others see the potential that he saw. Of course, even Devin could not make this project happen without the support of Selma Wilson and Cossy Pachares. So I'm thankful to them and the entire B&H team.

My friends, Jay and Kristi Smith at Juicebox Designs did design magic on the book cover and created distinctive beauty that will extend through the album and podcast covers as well as the website layout.

My parents, Bill and Hellen Kramp, trudged through my fourth book manuscript, proofreading, and making corrections as they have done for sixty years.

Finally, I would like to thank William Wilburforce. If you had not recorded your Psalm 119 experience in your journal in 1819, I would have never dreamed of beginning this journey.

John Kramp

Contents

Introduction

A Psalm 119 Experience

Watch out. Psalm 119 is about to sneak up and draw you into a life-changing experience.

Before long and without mental gymnastics, you'll remember all 176 verses of the longest chapter in the Bible. The 22 sections of this psalm will lock themselves into your mind and heart, changing forever the way you think about God's Word.

How can I declare this with confidence? It happened to me, and I have the memory of a gnat.

In fact, I was minding my own business when William Wilberforce told me about his experience with Psalm 119. Actually, that would have been creepy; the British politician who led the movement to abolish the slave trade died in 1833. His journal, though, tells the story. In 1819, Wilberforce wrote, "Walked from Hyde Park Corner repeating the 119th Psalm in great comfort."

The first time I read that statement, it startled me. Over the years I had read Psalm 119 and knew a bit about it. The structure of the psalm intrigued me—an acrostic poem using the twenty-two letters in the Hebrew alphabet. Writing a similar acrostic poem using the English alphabet would require eight lines beginning with "A" words, then eight lines beginning with "B" words, continuing through the alphabet and wrapping up with eight lines beginning with "Z" words.

Clearly, the writer wanted to remember this psalm and to help others remember it as well. The alphabetical acrostic provided a memory aid. I was impressed by the literary structure, but I could not imagine memorizing 176 verses. Everything changed as I began my *Psalm 119 Experience*.

The Tune in Your Head

While I cannot remember a 10-item shopping list in the minutes between my house and the store, I can recall and even sing (in private, thank you), all sorts of song lyrics stuck in my brain like lint over the years. That started me wondering—could I use music to memorize Psalm 119? It sounded like a long shot, but I decided to try.

I didn't want songs about the themes contained in Psalm 119; I wanted to remember all the words of Psalm 119. So I gave myself some rules as I began my adventure.

- I would write 22 songs, one for each of the 8-line sections of Psalm 119.
- Each song would include all the words from each section. My goal was to leave nothing out.
- Within each eight-line section, I could reorder the lines to find verses, a chorus, and a bridge. I wanted songs with a familiar structure, not chants.
- Repeating phrases and lines was acceptable, but I wanted to avoid reordering words within phrases.
- The songs should reflect the tone of the words in each section.
- The music for each of the 22 songs should be different, reflecting different styles that would aid memory.
- The songs should be simple enough for me to sing, which meant that I had about an 8-note range with which to work.

At the time I started, I had a demanding corporate job with very little time for extra projects. Out of necessity, I commandeered some time slots for song development—while shaving, while showering, while drying my hair, and during part of my commute to work. With no deadline in mind, I started, hoping songs would develop that would lock the words of Psalm 119 with tunes in my head.

Tell No One

Initially, I told no one, not even my wife, Lynn Marie. The whole idea of writing 22 songs to memorize Psalm 119 sounded odd. If you had told me that one day I would have the songs recorded and write a devotional book based on what I learned, I would have laughed. My experience back then was personal, private.

What I did not anticipate was the impact my *Psalm 119 Experience* would have on my life. As one song became five, and twelve songs grew into fifteen, then into twenty–two, the collective impact of having these words in my mind and heart began to change me.

- Psalm 119 songs became the soundtrack for my life. As I woke up in the morning, I hit "play" in my mind and began one of the songs, forcing my mind away from worries and setting my focus on God. As I went to sleep at night, I hit "play" once again and allowed particular songs to settle my anxious thoughts into sleep.

- The themes of the different Psalm 119 songs began to fortify me for things I was facing. Memorizing the psalm did what reading could never do—I understood the heartfelt themes the writer addressed and how God's Word equipped him for life.

- Since Psalm 119 is not attributed to a specific writer, it can be appropriated by anyone seeking God through His Word. This psalm became my psalm; these words became my words. Rather than professing God's Word is important, Psalm 119 helped me grasp that God's Word is my life.

- Wrestling with all the words in Psalm 119 through 22 sections helped me see that the writer had shared a personal testimony about a lifetime of living God's Word. From adolescence to maturity, he spoke with frank insight about the challenges and the conquests of life. His experiences challenged me to live with robust faith, anchored in God's Word, but not trivializing life's tough times with Bible-plaque platitudes.

At the halfway point in my *Psalm 119 Experience*, I hit a "crisis of belief" as Henry Blackaby described it in *Experiencing God*. I questioned whether I could complete the project and fretted that the whole thing was a silly distraction. My wife, along with my friend Greg Nelson, stepped into my faith void and encouraged me to keep going. I did. And one day it happened; the 22 song was complete. No one was more surprised than me.

From Personal to Public Experiences

After months of nurturing my own heart with the songs that grew from my *Psalm 119 Experience*, I had the opportunity to share a few of them with a larger group. Although I had written songs, played the guitar, and sung publicly years ago, I was never really good, at best one of the fastest in the slow group. Years and perspective had helped me make peace with the level of gifts God had given me, and I had determined not to inflict an audience with my singing again. But something changed. When the opportunity came, I wanted to share some of the Psalm 119 songs with this group, not for me, but for them. God had impacted my life so powerfully, I felt compelled to tell the story, to share some of what God had taught me. And so I did.

Most people are kind, especially in the South. This is the home of "heart blessings." So as I sang my songs that day, people could say, "Bless his heart." The uninitiated might comment, "Isn't that sweet. Look how supportive they are." The truth is that a Southern "heart blessing" means "God help him; he's doing the best he can."

When I talked about my *Psalm 119 Experience* that day and sang a few of the songs, people engaged. The lights were up; I could see people's faces. They listened and responded. That's when I began to wonder if others could have a *Psalm 119 Experience* as well.

I began thinking about a devotional book with short writings based on each of the 22 Psalm 119 songs, focused on the phrases and themes. Later, I dreamed of a recording that would draw on the strengths of professional musicians to transform my feeble efforts into music that people could listen to, allowing the words of Psalm 119 to wedge into their minds and hearts.

Your Psalm 119 Experience

What you hold in your hands or are reading on your phone or tablet is an invitation. More than likely, you cannot imagine memorizing the longest chapter in the Bible. Here's the good news: you don't need to pursue that goal. In fact, I suggest that you do not set out to memorize Psalm 119. Instead, set out to experience it.

Begin using the devotional, reading a short section each day. Once you work through all the sections, begin again.

Download the songs from iTunes and begin listening in your car or on whatever device you use. Remember the songs are designed to be sticky, like hot gum in your brain, not necessarily your favorite musical style. See if the words begin to lodge in your brain so you can draw on them as needed.

How will you know you're having a *Psalm 119 Experience?* Here are a few positive indicators to anticipate.

- In a difficult circumstance, do the words of a particular Psalm 119 song come to mind? If so, pay attention and allow those truths to fortify your heart.
- Do you struggle to control your thoughts as you wake up or go to sleep? Intentionally think about one of

the songs, letting the words set your mind on a God-ward plane, moving you out of a downward spiral of despair.

- When a circumstance in your life surprises you, draw on one of the Psalm 119 songs to settle your heart, protecting you from reactions you'll regret.
- Capitalize on your "mindless" times to focus on God's Word. Reclaim your time in the shower, driving to work, shopping, working out, whatever else you do as part of ongoing life. Transform "mindless" time to discipleship time.
- Read through Psalm 119 in its entirety. Don't allow songs and other tools to distract you from interacting directly with God's Word. The more you read this section of God's Word, the more deeply it will impact you.

You'll notice that I used the Holman Christian Standard Bible (HCSB) for this *Psalm 119 Experience*. Since I was trying to write songs with each of the 22 sections, I needed a translation that captured the poetry of the text without drifting into paraphrase. Using different Bible translations is a privilege and a blessing. Find the Bible that fits your needs. Even if you've never used the HCSB before, I think you'll enjoy using it for this *Psalm 119 Experience* as I did.

What Comes Next

What do you suppose prompted William Wilberforce to quote Psalm 119 on his walk from Hyde Park Corner that day in 1819? History tells us about the struggles he faced in his quest to abolish the British slave trade. Critics confronted him. Power brokers accosted him. Friends betrayed him. His health failed. At times, his faith faltered. That day, though, he reflected on the power of God's Word through the words of Psalm 119. Certainly, he needed God's power that day. So do we.

Without God's Word we could never know God. Given thousands of guesses, we could not imagine the truth of the gospel on our own. God revealed so we could know. God speaks now through what God has spoken in His Word. Psalm 119 invites us to a deeper experience with God through a deeper experience with His Word.

Perhaps one day you'll note in your journal, "Drove to work quoting Psalm 119 in great comfort."

John Kramp
Brentwood, Tennessee
2014

Chapter 1

Blameless Way

How happy are those whose way is blameless, who live according to the law of the LORD!

Happy are those who keep His decrees and seek Him with all their heart.

They do nothing wrong; they follow His ways.

You have commanded that Your precepts be diligently kept.

If only my ways were committed to keeping Your statutes!

Then I would not be ashamed when I think about all Your commands.

I will praise You with a sincere heart when I learn Your righteous judgments.

I will keep Your statutes; never abandon me.

—Psalm 119:1–8

Day 1

Blameless

How happy are those whose way is blameless, who live according to the law of the LORD! (Ps. 119:1)

If you seek a happy life, discover the secret to a blameless life. Impossible? Can any of us stand before God innocent of wrongdoing, free of guilt and not subject to blame? No. At least not on our own. But God provided a way to the impossible.

Once you were alienated and hostile in your minds because of your evil actions. But now He has reconciled you by His physical body through His death, to present you holy, faultless, and blameless before Him. (Col. 1:21–22)

Our only hope for a blameless life was to be credited with Jesus' perfect life. We were hopelessly alienated from God. But God opened the door marked "impossible" with a gospel key. We traded our guilt for His perfection. Although stunningly sinful, we received new standing before God. In Christ, God welcomed us just as if we had never sinned. We were justified.

Our new life empowered by God made it possible for our way of life to change.

Now may the God of peace Himself sanctify you completely. And may your spirit, soul, and body be kept sound and blameless for the coming of our Lord Jesus Christ. (1 Thess. 5:23)

Having granted us blameless status before Him, God began the ongoing work of transforming us. Through His Spirit living within us, He is working in us powerfully to change how we think, what we value, and what we do. As our internal life changes, our external way of life changes. We live according to God's instruction, His Word. As we do, we discover profound contentment, and satisfaction. We experience godly happiness.

Following God's instruction, His Word, points us to Christ, the only way we can be blameless before God. Considered blameless by God, everything is different in our lives now and in eternity. God shattered the sad way of sin and gave us the happiness of right standing with Him forever.

Day 2

Seeking

Happy are those who keep His decrees and seek Him with all their heart. (Ps. 119:2)

What are you keeping? What are you seeking? Our answers to those questions impact the course of our lives.

To keep God's decrees, His authoritative orders, we must know God's Word. Knowing precedes keeping. We cannot keep what we do not know. So our discipleship priority is to know what God has revealed to us in the Bible. Our keeping displays our loving.

"If you love Me, you will keep My commands." (John 14:15)

We cannot say we love Jesus without knowing and keeping His Word. But knowing biblical facts cannot become an end; it must remain a means. God gave us His Word so that we could know Him.

You will seek Me and find Me when you search for Me with all your heart. (Jer. 29:13)

Heads stuffed with biblical facts can produce dangerous minds if not focused on a growing, vibrant relationship with Jesus.

So if you have been raised with the Messiah, seek what is above, where the Messiah is, seated at the right hand of God. Set your minds on what is above, not on what is on the earth. For you have died, and your life is hidden with the Messiah in God. (Col. 3:1–3)

God places in our hearts the desire to seek Him. Left to our own inclinations, we poke for trinkets. Thankfully, God seeks us so that we can seek Him. God works in our hearts. Only then can we seek Him with all our hearts. Once set in motion, seeking to know God more and keeping His Word becomes our happy pursuit.

Day 3

Ways

They do nothing wrong; they follow His ways. You have commanded that Your precepts be diligently kept. (Ps. 119:3–4)

We discover the ways of God by studying what He has revealed about Himself in His Word. There we learn how He acts and why, what He values, what He judges, and what He desires of us. It is possible to learn God's Word yet fail to learn God's ways. His ways encompass all that God has said and done, a discernable pattern that we can follow. Moses learned the ways of God.

He revealed His ways to Moses, His deeds to the people of Israel. (Ps. 103:7)

The people focused on God's deeds, what He did, but never understood His ways. Like them, we can know much about God by mastering an array of Bible facts yet fail to understand God's ways. God's Word can become a rule book.

As we learn God's ways, we understand the joy of His commands. The Ten Commandments become a field of freedom, not a tiny fenced yard. God's commands and precepts show us how to live to please God and to experience life fully.

So keep the commands of the LORD your God by walking in His ways and fearing Him. (Deut. 8:6)

Because of our awe of God and what He has done for us in Christ, we desire to do what He commands. We strive with diligence to keep His precepts, persisting and applying effort as God gives us strength, grateful all the while that God is working in us.

For it is God who is working in you, enabling you both to desire and to work out His good purpose. (Phil. 2:13)

Day 4

Shame

If only my ways were committed to keeping Your statutes! Then I would not be ashamed when I think about all Your commands. (Ps. 119:5–6)

Discovering God's ways reveals all that is lacking in our ways. In spite of the good work that God has begun in us, we falter and fail. Our ways, the patterns of our lives, run helter–skelter. With wistful longing we imagine how much better life could be.

We know that God aligns us constantly. His Word gives us statutes, a clear path for obedience. Our dream, though, is that we could move beyond occasional obedience. We want to be committed. No, that's not quite right. We want new desires.

Take delight in the LORD, and He will give you your heart's desires. (Ps. 37:4)

How much easier life would be if we desired all that God desires for us. Oh, to delight in Him and in His Word. Oh, to be done with exhausting shame each time we fail. Fortunately, Jesus dealt with our shame.

Keeping our eyes on Jesus, the source and perfecter of our faith, who for the joy that lay before Him endured a cross and despised the shame and has sat down at the right hand of God's throne. (Heb. 12:2)

Jesus suffered shame for us so that we could think about His commands with only gratitude. Yes, we fail, but we confess our sin and experience forgiveness.

If we confess our sins, He is faithful and righteous to forgive us our sins and to cleanse us from all unrighteousness. (1 John 1:9)

God's commands remind us that without Jesus, it would have been impossible for us to measure up to God's standards. We feel shame because we have behaved shamefully. Striving to measure up would have never been enough; we needed a sacrifice. We were sinking in sin; God gave us a Savior.

Our ways end at the cross. The cross ends our shame.

Day 5

Abandoned

I will praise You with a sincere heart when I learn Your righteous judgments. I will keep Your statutes; never abandon me. (Ps. 119:7–8)

Connections matter. Sequence matters.

Here's an example. Righteous judgments. Learning. A sincere heart. Praise.

All are connected in a sequence. God has revealed His righteous judgments in His Word. He gives us the privilege of studying His Word and learning what it says. The more we learn about God, the more God changes our hearts as He works in us through His Holy Spirit. In light of all this, we must praise Him.

Praise the God and Father of our Lord Jesus Christ. According to His great mercy, He has given us a new birth into a living hope through the resurrection of Jesus Christ from the dead. (1 Pet. 1:3)

Here's another series. Keeping God's statutes. God's not abandoning us.

What's the connection? What's the sequence? If God's ongoing work in our lives depended on us keeping His statutes, we would be lost. We must think the other way around. God keeps us so that we can keep His statutes.

"I give them eternal life, and they will never perish—ever! No one will snatch them out of My hand. My Father, who has given them to Me, is greater than all. No one is able to snatch them out of the Father's hand." (John 10:28–29)

Focusing on God's Word prompts us to praise. We praise God for the change He has made in our hearts. We praise Him for His righteous judgments satisfied through the death of Christ. We praise Him for the desire He has placed within us to keep His statutes.

Praise is a reflexive privilege for God's children. Hearts changed by God take the words God has revealed then speak those truths back to Him. We are freed from fear and secure in His love. No longer terrified by death, we are free to live and live to praise. God never abandons us.

Blameless Way
Psalm 119:1–8

Verse 1

How happy are those whose way is blameless,
who live according to the law of the LORD!
Happy are those who keep His decrees
and seek Him with all their heart.
They do nothing wrong; they follow His ways.
You have commanded that Your precepts be diligently kept.

Verse 2

If only my ways, my ways were committed,
committed to keeping Your statutes!
Then I would not be ashamed
when I think about all Your commands.
I will praise You with a sincere heart,
when I learn your righteous judgments.
I will keep your statutes; never abandon me.

Close

How happy are those whose way is blameless
Who live according to the law of the LORD.[1]

---

1. You can download this and all songs in the *Psalm 119 Experience* from iTunes. See page 245 for more information.

Chapter 2

Pure Through God's Word

How can a young man keep his way pure? By keeping Your word.

I have sought You with all my heart; don't let me wander from Your commands.

I have treasured Your word in my heart so that I may not sin against You.

LORD, may You be praised; teach me Your statutes.

With my lips I proclaim all the judgments from Your mouth.

I rejoice in the way revealed by Your decrees as much as in all riches.

I will meditate on Your precepts and think about Your ways.

I will delight in Your statutes; I will not forget Your word.

—Psalm 119:9–16

Day 1

Pure

How can a young man keep his way pure? By keeping Your word. (Ps. 119:9)

Having been forgiven of our sins in Christ, we are pure before God. It is as if someone switched the charts in the doctor's office, replacing the record of an elderly emphysema patient with that of a teenage athlete. When we stand before God, He will not measure us based on our record of personal achievement. So why pursue a life of moral purity now? Because we want to enjoy deeper fellowship with God in our daily lives.

"The pure in heart are blessed, for they will see God." (Matt. 5:8)

Having been freed from the penalty of sin, why would we willingly wallow in its filth? Because of God's mercy toward us, we desire to live distinctive lives.

So that you may be blameless and pure, children of God who are faultless in a crooked and perverted generation, among whom you shine like stars in the world. (Phil. 2:15)

We have wised up to sin's tricks. We know that it promises but never delivers, entices but only teases. Sin promises to add, but it only dilutes, mixing foulness with our souls until we live clouded lives. Like one who has ingested poison, we counteract sin's influence with God's Word.

Like newborn infants, desire the pure spiritual milk, so that you may grow by it for your salvation, since you have tasted that the Lord is good. (1 Pet. 2:2–3)

God's Word adds strength so we can resist sin's seduction. The struggle for purity is not limited to young men. All of us struggle, irrespective of age or gender. Age, though, brings at least one advantage: we learn the wisdom of running from sin.

Flee from youthful passions, and pursue righteousness, faith, love, and peace, along with those who call on the Lord from a pure heart. (2 Tim. 2:22)

This is a hard, fallen world in which to live. With the wisdom of God's Word and God's Spirit working within us, we can live with increasing purity.

Day 2

Wandering

I have sought You with all my heart; don't let me wander from Your commands. (Ps. 119:10)

An honest examination reveals a paradox: we seek God; we wander from God. Having begun a relationship of grace with God through Jesus' work for us, we want to experience more of Him. Having realized the gruesome cost of sin, we want no more to do with it. Our impulse is to run from sin and run to God. Yet at other times, we walk away from God while looking back at Him over one shoulder.

One of the residual impacts of sin is wandering. Before Christ, we could do nothing else. We were like the ancient wanderers Jeremiah described.

This is what the LORD says concerning these people: Truly they love to wander; they never rest their feet. So the LORD does not accept them. Now He will remember their guilt and punish their sins. (Jer. 14:10)

Christians throughout the years have lamented this propensity to wander. In 1758, Robert Robinson included the following words in a collection of hymns:

O to grace how great a debtor daily I'm constrained to be! Let Thy goodness, like a fetter, bind my wandering heart to Thee. Prone to wander, Lord, I feel it, prone to leave the God I love; Here's my heart, O take and seal it, seal it for Thy courts above.

One evidence of God's work in us is our heart's desire to seek Him, to know His commands and follow them. God's Word clarifies the destructive impact of sin. When we are thinking clearly, we want nothing to do with sin.

For the love of money is a root of all kinds of evil, and by craving it, some have wandered away from the faith and pierced themselves with many pains. (1 Tim. 6:10)

Because of sin, Christ was pierced for us. Why would we now willfully walk toward sin's sharp point? So we pray, "Oh, God, bind our wandering hearts to Thee."

Day 3

Treasured

I have treasured Your word in my heart so that I may not sin against You. LORD, may You be praised; teach me Your statutes. (Ps. 119:11–12)

To counteract the wearying pull of sin, we intensify our focus on God's Word. In ways we cannot fully explain, exposing our minds to God's Word fortifies us to resist sin. When sin tugs at us with the greatest intensity, we remain anchored. What we treasure reveals our heart.

*For where your treasure is, there your heart will be also.
(Matt. 6:21)*

To keep track of your treasure, keep track of your heart. So
is it possible as a Christian not to sin? Yes and no.

*My little children, I am writing you these things so that you
may not sin. But if anyone does sin, we have an advocate
with the Father—Jesus Christ the Righteous One. (1 John
2:1)*

We gain nothing by considering sin inevitable. Why think
of ourselves as victims when God has equipped us to battle
sin's enticements? God gave us His Word so that we would
not sin. That's the good news. God gave us an advocate for
when we sin. That is even better news.

The more we treasure God's Word in our hearts, the more
we can resist sin. We will recognize sin's seduction early and
escape quickly. When tripped up by sin, we can confess to
Jesus, our advocate, immediately and experience restored fellowship without delay.

*Now we have this treasure in clay jars, so that this extraor-
dinary power may be from God and not from us. (2 Cor.
4:7)*

God's work in our lives is a treasure. The reality, though,
is that we are frail, fragile. We are clay pots easily shattered.
Fortunately, God knows our nature. He does not rely on us to
protect what He has given us freely by grace. God guards His
work. He gives us the privilege of praise. Clay pots become
treasure chests, and God alone receives glory.

Day 4

Proclaiming

With my lips I proclaim all the judgments from Your mouth.
(Ps. 119:13)

There is power in proclamation. As those who follow
Christ and know His Word, we speak about Him to others.
We announce what we have learned and explain what we have
experienced. We declare what matters most to us, this reality
that God has revealed in His Word. We have discovered His
judgments, His authoritative statements to all people in all
places at all times. We must speak.

Proclamation is our responsibility and our privilege.
Through all the stages of our lives we talk with others about
the good news—God's gospel work, His gracious work of
transforming enemies into children of God. This was King
David's testimony:

God, You have taught me from my youth, and I still pro-
claim Your wonderful works. (Ps. 71:17)

Even when I am old and gray, God, do not abandon me.
Then I will proclaim Your power to another generation,
Your strength to all who are to come. (Ps. 71:18)

The judgments God has made known in His Word are not
interesting facts; they are truth to be spoken with urgency.
This is the work to which God has called us and for which
He empowers us.

We proclaim Him, warning and teaching everyone with all
wisdom, so that we may present everyone mature in Christ.
I labor for this, striving with His strength that works power-
fully in me. (Col. 1:28–29)

As we speak to others, we speak to our own hearts. The more we proclaim, the stronger the truth grows in us. We live as heralds, announcing the good news of our great God.

> *How beautiful on the mountains are the feet of the herald, who proclaims peace, who brings news of good things, who proclaims salvation, who says to Zion, "Your God reigns!" (Isa. 52:7)*

Day 5

Rejoicing

> *I rejoice in the way revealed by Your decrees as much as in all riches. (Ps. 119:14)*

Knowing God's Word helps us resist sin, cling to God, discover treasure, and proclaim good news gladly. Why would we not rejoice? The apostle Paul did and exhorted others to join him.

> *Rejoice in the Lord always. I will say it again: Rejoice! (Phil. 4:4)*

Rejoicing goes hand in hand with discovering. When recovering something of value, we express joy and relief. How much more when we find a gem infinitely beyond our means! The reality, though, is that with spiritual things, we could not rejoice if God had not chosen to reveal.

> *The hidden things belong to the LORD our God, but the revealed things belong to us and our children forever, so that we may follow all the words of this law. (Deut. 29:29)*

> *But now revealed and made known through the prophetic Scriptures, according to the command of the eternal God to*

advance the obedience of faith among all nations. (Rom. 16:26)

Why do we see and value what others consider trivial? Are we wiser than others? Have we intellectual prowess? Do we alone recognize the priceless among the knickknacks? Of course not. We see because God has opened our eyes to His incredible truth.

Once a priceless artifact has been verified, its value is evident. Even the untrained speak of its worth after the fact, while earlier they passed it by without a glance. So it is with spiritual riches. Jesus warned against placing too high a valuation on temporal things while underestimating the true value of the eternal.

"That's how it is with the one who stores up treasure for himself and is not rich toward God." (Luke 12:21)

We see with spiritual eyes. We rejoice with changed hearts. We trade our lives for true riches.

Oh, the depth of the riches both of the wisdom and the knowledge of God! How unsearchable His judgments and untraceable His ways! (Rom. 11:33)

Pure Through God's Word
Psalm 119:9–16

Verse 1

How can a young man keep his way pure?
By keeping Your word.
I have sought You with all my heart;
don't let me wander from Your commands.

Chorus

I have treasured Your word in my heart so that I may not sin against You.

LORD, may You be praised; teach me Your statutes.

With my lips I proclaim all the judgments from Your mouth.

I have treasured Your word in my heart so that I may not sin against You.

Verse 2

I will meditate on Your precepts and think on Your ways.

I will delight in Your statutes;

I will not forget, forget Your word.

Repeat Chorus

Bridge

I rejoice in the way revealed by Your decrees as much as in all riches.

Close

How can a young man keep his way pure? By keeping Your word.

How can we all keep our way pure? By keeping Your word.

Chapter 3

Wonderful Things in Your Law

Deal generously with Your servant so that I might live; then I will keep Your word.

Open my eyes so that I may see wonderful things in Your law.

I am a stranger on earth; do not hide Your commands from me.

I am continually overcome by longing for Your judgments.

You rebuke the proud, the accursed, who wander from Your commands.

Take insult and contempt away from me, for I have kept Your decrees.

Though princes sit together speaking against me, Your servant will think about Your statutes;

Your decrees are my delight and my counselors.

—Psalm 119:17–24

Day 1

Generous

Deal generously with Your servant so that I might live; then I will keep Your word. (Ps. 119:17)

How should we expect God to treat us? He is the ultimate Lord; we are mere servants. If our world were an old English household with lords and ladies, we would be the downstairs staff. Yet God upended the established order and granted us privileged access.

Therefore let us approach the throne of grace with boldness, so that we may receive mercy and find grace to help us at the proper time. (Heb. 4:16)

Audacious but true—we can approach God with boldness because He said we could. We can seek mercy from Him and receive it. We can request help. In His grace, at the proper time, He will help us. Slowly the truth becomes clear: God is dealing with us in an unexpected manner.

I will sing to the LORD because He has treated me generously. (Ps. 13:6)

What a shocking turn of events. As we consider all that God did for us, we struggle to find apt descriptive words. Grace. Mercy. Love. Kindness. Yes, these and more. But in all of these, God's portions to us have been generous—liberal, openhanded, ample, and marked by abundance. God's generosity is not limited to His past dealings with us. We continue to ask, and He continues to give abundantly based on our specific needs.

Now if any of you lacks wisdom, he should ask God, who gives to all generously and without criticizing, and it will be given to him. (James 1:5)

Selfish interests do not drive our requests for generosity. We need God's generous portion so that we can keep His Word. Stingy living is inconceivable for those who have received abundantly.

Remember this: The person who sows sparingly will also reap sparingly, and the person who sows generously will also reap generously. (2 Cor. 9:6)

We serve a generous God, so we live as generous people. There is no other appropriate option.

Day 2

Wonderful

Open my eyes so that I may see wonderful things in Your law. (Ps. 119:18)

God's Word provides a living record of God's wonder. We look at His law and marvel at its order. We read what God revealed in the Old Testament and fulfilled in Christ and shake our heads at the scope of this truth. What we see must be declared with our lips.

Declare His glory among the nations, His wonderful works among all peoples. (1 Chron. 16:24)

LORD my God, You have done many things—Your wonderful works and Your plans for us; none can compare with You. If I were to report and speak of them, they are more than can be told. (Ps. 40:5)

The sad truth though is that we read of God's wonders and experience His work in our lives and sometimes respond with a yawn. Worse yet, we can rebel against the God of wonder.

Our fathers in Egypt did not grasp the significance of Your wonderful works or remember Your many acts of faithful love; instead, they rebelled by the sea—the Red Sea. (Ps. 106:7)

During Jesus' earthly ministry, He wove his life among a tapestry of people, rich and poor, religious and irreligious. Drawing from an Old Testament reference, Jesus taught that He was the cornerstone that God had provided.

Jesus said to them, "Have you never read in the Scriptures: The stone that the builders rejected has become the cornerstone. This came from the Lord and is wonderful in our eyes?" (Matt. 21:42)

In those days, most who looked failed to see. They rejected the cornerstone. May we not fall into such folly and fail to recognize God's wonder among us.

Day 3

Hidden

I am a stranger on earth; do not hide Your commands from me. I am continually overcome by longing for Your judgments. (Ps. 119:19–20)

As Christians, we are displaced in this current world. We live topsy-turvy, driving on the wrong side while people honk and glare. We are resident aliens passing through to our eternal homeland. In our disorientation, connecting with God through His Word becomes our priority.

Desperately, continually, we probe God's Word, searching His commands for how to set things right. At times, our great need meets silence. It's as if God is hiding from us what we need. Other "strangers" have shared this experience.

LORD, why do You stand so far away? Why do You hide in times of trouble? (Ps. 10:1)

Imagine two sides of one door. On our side, it seems as if God is hiding things from us. From God's side, the reality is more complex. God knows that when we feel like strangers on earth, when we puzzle over things, and when we long continually for Him, we gain strength. The only way for us to survive this alien earthly life is to maintain a laser focus on God. We find an example in the prophet Daniel.

So the king gave the order, and they brought Daniel and threw him into the lions' den. The king said to Daniel, "May your God, whom you serve continually, rescue you!" (Dan. 6:16)

Daniel's pattern of longing for God was so clear that an unbelieving despot recognized it. Over years in exile, Daniel had learned that God alone provided the truth, commands, and judgments needed to navigate chronic confusion.

He reveals the deep and hidden things; He knows what is in the darkness, and light dwells with Him. (Dan. 2:22)

Living too easily in this world sounds a warning siren for sojourners. That shrill noise prompts a rush for shelter. There we wait for God to make clear what has seemed hidden, knowing only He can satisfy our longings.

Day 4

Pride

You rebuke the proud, the accursed, who wander from Your commands. Take insult and contempt away from me, for I have kept Your decrees. (Ps. 119:21–22)

Nothing good comes to the proud, at least from a spiritual perspective.

God resists the proud, but gives grace to the humble. (James 4:6)

Why would we put ourselves in a posture that God has declared He will resist? Living with pride is insane. Become proud and get ready to tumble.

Pride comes before destruction, and an arrogant spirit before a fall. (Prov. 16:18)

Before his downfall a man's heart is proud, but humility comes before honor. (Prov. 18:12)

Living around proud people is a pain. They insult others, speaking with disdain and disrespect. Proud people treat others with contempt, acting as if others are beneath consideration.

The paradox of pride is that we can see it clearly in others and miss its ugly reality in our own lives. Pride is insidious. Carelessness and pride bloom like dandelions. We must fight back, or we will lose control. God's Word, His clear commands, and His concise decrees, prepare us for battle by instructing us through positive and negative examples.

Jesus warned us that people would treat us poorly, the same way they treated Him. We should consider such belittling a badge of honor.

You are blessed when people hate you, when they exclude you, insult you, and slander your name as evil because of the Son of Man. (Luke 6:22)

God has chosen sides on the issue of pride. He will rebuke the proud, confronting their insults and contemptuous behavior. The great flip-flop is coming; the top goes down, the bottom comes up. For now, we endure the prideful while using them as a mirror to reveal our own pride. Oddly, we react most fiercely to traits in others we tolerate in ourselves. Let our greatest vigil against pride focus on the preening pride strutting in our own hearts.

Day 5

Entourage

Though princes sit together speaking against me, Your servant will think about Your statutes; Your decrees are my delight and my counselors. (Ps. 119:23–24)

Know any princes? Most of us don't, but we know their kind: people in positions for reasons other than competence, people kept in positions through relationships. Princes often have time on their hands, so they enjoy coffee breaks with other princely folks. Often they evaluate non-princely people, find them deficient, and discuss their inadequacies. It's no fun being around princes. So how is a non-prince to survive?

Remember to Whom you report. The princes may believe you are at their beck and call. Not true. You are a servant of the true King.

Remember the truth your King has shared with you. He has given you His statutes and decrees. Your King has made His will known. If the princes in your life contradict the King, stand your ground and trust your King to defend you.

Another irritating thing about princes is that they travel with an entourage, a group of toady yes-people who live in reflected glory. If dealing with princes is bad, dealing with toadies is worse.

Do you ever wish you had an entourage? Would it be fun to be considered an important person surrounded by others waiting for you to snap your fingers? Actually, a clutch of lackeys would poison your spiritual life.

If an entourage is out, what about a board of directors? How about a team to give you counsel, to keep you out of trouble, and to make sure your life stays on course? We can have that kind of board. God's statutes and decrees along with all that He has revealed in His Word become our counselors.

Stop fretting about the princes. Who cares what they say about you. Focus on what God says about you. You are His servant. Delight in Him.

Wonderful Things in Your Law
Psalm 119:17–24

Chorus

Deal generously with Your servant so that I might live;
then I will keep Your word.
Open my eyes so that I may see
wonderful things in Your law.

Verse 1

I am a stranger on earth; do not hide Your commands from me.
I am continually overcome by longing for Your judgments.

Repeat Chorus

Verse 2

You rebuke the proud, the accursed, who wander from Your commands.
Take insult, contempt away from me, for I have kept Your decrees.

Bridge

Though princes sit together speaking against me,
Your servant will think about Your statutes; Your decrees
Your decrees are my delight and my counselors.

Chorus

Deal generously with Your servant so that I might live;
then I will keep Your word.
Open my eyes so that I may see
wonderful things in Your law.
Wonderful things from Your law.

Chapter 4

Life Through Your Word

My life is down in the dust; give me life through Your word.

I told You about my life, and You listened to me; teach me Your statutes.

Help me understand the meaning of Your precepts so that I can meditate on Your wonders.

I am weary from grief; strengthen me through Your word.

Keep me from the way of deceit, and graciously give me Your instruction.

I have chosen the way of truth; I have set Your ordinances before me.

I cling to Your decrees; LORD, do not put me to shame.

I pursue the way of Your commands, for You broaden my understanding.

—Psalm 119:25–32

Day 1

Down

My life is down in the dust; give me life through Your word.
(Ps. 119:25)

You may not care for the blues as a musical form, but sometimes that's the music that matches the mood. You get knocked down, pressed down. Strong hands grind your face in the dust. You gasp. Listen closely and you may hear a driving bass, a wailing guitar, and a voice cracked by hard living. Don't panic. It's just the blues.

If the Bible had a soundtrack, it would include some blues tracks. All sorts of people in the Bible were down low and looking up.

For we have sunk down to the dust; our bodies cling to the
ground. Rise up! Help us! Redeem us because of Your faith-
ful love. (Ps. 44:25–26)

When you're eating dust, you've got to get help. You're short of breath and need air to survive. God's Word explains where to turn.

All Scripture is inspired by God. (2 Tim. 3:16)

The word *inspired* means "God-breathed." Reading the Bible is like divine CPR. Of course, this is how life began.

Then the LORD God formed the man out of the dust from
the ground and breathed the breath of life into his nostrils,
and the man became a living being. (Gen. 2:7)

We come from dust. We're heading back to dust. So when our lives are down in the dust we need the breath of God from His Word of life. Relax. Read. Breathe.

Day 2

Telling

I told You about my life, and You listened to me; teach me Your statutes. Help me understand the meaning of Your precepts so that I can meditate on Your wonders. (Ps. 119:26–27)

Life sours if we hold things in that need to come out. The fastest way out of the dust is prayer that connects us with God.

LORD, You have heard the desire of the humble; You will strengthen their hearts. You will listen carefully. (Ps. 10:17)

It's good to tell God about our lives. Holding nothing back, we express our deepest fears and needs. But we don't indulge in dump-truck praying, simply emptying our load on God without hearing what He has to say. We pray purposefully. We want God to use His Word to teach us His statutes, help us understand His precepts, and enable us to meditate on His wonders.

Talking is our side of prayer; the Bible is God's side. He answers by helping us discover portions of Scripture that address our needs, especially the examples of many in the Bible who passed through extreme difficulties with faith.

Jesus exhorted His disciples to pray, emphasizing the "when" and not the "if" of prayer.

But when you pray, go into your private room, shut your door, and pray to your Father who is in secret. And your Father who sees in secret will reward you. (Matt. 6:6)

We tell God about our lives, and He listens to us. In return, we meditate on the wonder that God speaks to us through

His Word. Prayer becomes an uplifting conversation for people who are down.

Day 3

Weary

I am weary from grief; strengthen me through Your word. (Ps. 119:28)

We get tired every day. We don't necessarily get weary every day. Weariness comes after excessive exertion, a level of "tired" that cannot be hidden. During His earthly ministry, Jesus expressed compassion for the weary.

"Come to Me, all of you who are weary and burdened, and I will give you rest." (Matt. 11:28)

After Jesus told His disciples He would be killed, He took them to a garden to pray. After pulling away from them for personal prayer, He returned to find them sleeping.

When He got up from prayer and came to the disciples, He found them sleeping, exhausted from their grief. (Luke 22:45)

There is perhaps no "weary" like grief weary. Grief overcame the disciples' intention to pray. Weariness wore them out as it does us. So what can we do? God in His grace personally empowers us in our weariness.

Now the God of all grace, who called you to His eternal glory in Christ Jesus, will personally restore, establish, strengthen, and support you after you have suffered a little. (1 Pet. 5:10)

God's recharging tool for our lives is His Word, giving us perspective on weariness and grief.

He will wipe away every tear from their eyes. Death will no longer exist; grief, crying, and pain will exist no longer, because the previous things have passed away. (Rev. 21:4)

We know the future. Weariness and grief have a term limit. God gives us strength to outlast both.

Day 4

Choices

Keep me from the way of deceit, and graciously give me Your instruction. I have chosen the way of truth; I have set Your ordinances before me. (Ps. 119:29–30)

When we are down, alternative paths look appealing. Renegades from God seem to travel with impunity. They have chosen a path of deceit described by others in the Bible.

See, the wicked one is pregnant with evil, conceives trouble, and gives birth to deceit. (Ps. 7:14)

God sees what they do and has registered His displeasure.

Woe to those who drag wickedness with cords of deceit and pull sin along with cart ropes. (Isa. 5:18)

"Woe" is biblical language for, "Watch out; you're going to get it." That's why we don't envy the wicked. God has graciously given us instructions. We know how things work and the consequences packaged with choices. Why would we go toward that which God says "woe"?

The LORD is good and upright; therefore He shows sinners the way. He leads the humble in what is right and teaches them His way. All the LORD's ways show faithful love and truth to those who keep His covenant and decrees. (Ps. 25:8–10)

There is a way of truth, an open path. God's ordinances, the authoritative decrees in His Word, mark the way.

Your eyes will see your Teacher, and whenever you turn to the right or to the left, your ears will hear this command behind you: "This is the way. Walk in it." (Isa. 30:20–21)

It is a privilege to choose the way of truth. Apart from God's gracious work of first speaking His truth to us through His Word, we could have never made that choice.

Day 5

Clinging

I cling to Your decrees; LORD, do not put me to shame. I pursue the way of Your commands, for You broaden my understanding. (Ps. 119:31–32)

When our worlds get rocked, we must find something secure. We reach and then clutch. With arms wrapped around the unmoving, we hold on until life stops shaking.

For the Christian, God's Word is the pylon to which we cling during the storm. God's decrees, His authoritative orders, cannot be moved, so we stake our future on them.

Many people reach for the wrong things, failing to perceive their folly. The prophet Jonah noted their experience and contrasted it with the right way.

Those who cling to worthless idols forsake faithful love, but as for me, I will sacrifice to You with a voice of thanksgiving.

I will fulfill what I have vowed. Salvation is from the LORD! (Jon. 2:8–9)

Others may jeer at our clinging, but we rely on the Lord for confirmation. By faith, we will not be shamed by choosing to trust God. Our goal, though, is not to remain in place; we seek to move on with God. We pursue a deeper knowledge of God's commands.

Then you will understand righteousness, justice, and integrity—every good path. For wisdom will enter your mind, and knowledge will delight your heart. Discretion will watch over you, and understanding will guard you. (Prov. 2:9–11)

Over time, God broadens our understanding of His Word. Our grasp of truth expands as our foundation becomes increasingly strong.

According to the riches of His grace that He lavished on us with all wisdom and understanding. (Eph. 1:7–8)

God lavished grace on us, grace to know Him and grace to understand His Word. Those who are wise cling with confidence.

Life Through Your Word
Psalm 119:25–32

Chorus

My life is down, my life is down in the dust; give me, give me, life through Your word.

My life is down, my life down in the dust; give me life through Your word.

Verse 1

I told You about my life, and You listened to me; teach me Your statutes.

Help me understand the meaning of Your precepts so that I can meditate on Your wonders.

I am weary from grief; strengthen me through Your word.

Repeat Chorus

My life is down, my life is down in the dust; give me, give me, life through Your word.

My life is down, my life down in the dust; give me life through Your word.

Verse 2

Keep me from the way of deceit, and graciously give me, give me Your instruction.

I have chosen the way of truth; I have set Your ordinances before me.

I cling to Your decrees; LORD, do not put me to shame.

Bridge

I pursue the way of Your commands, for You broaden my understanding.

I pursue the way of Your commands, for You broaden my understanding.

Final Chorus

My life is down, my life is down in the dust; give me, give me, life through Your word.

My life is down, my life down in the dust; give me life through Your word.

Give me life through your word. Give me life through Your word.

Chapter 5

Give Me Life in Your Ways

Teach me, LORD, the meaning of Your statutes, and I will always keep them.

Help me understand Your instruction, and I will obey it and follow it with all my heart.

Help me stay on the path of Your commands, for I take pleasure in it.

Turn my heart to Your decrees and not to material gain.

Turn my eyes from looking at what is worthless; give me life in Your ways.

Confirm what You said to Your servant, for it produces reverence for You.

Turn away the disgrace I dread; indeed, Your judgments are good.

How I long for Your precepts! Give me life through Your righteousness.

—Psalm 119:33–40

Day 1

Teach

Teach me, LORD, the meaning of Your statutes, and I will always keep them. Help me understand Your instruction, and I will obey it and follow it with all my heart. (Ps. 119:33–34)

Learning from a master teacher is a privilege. Learning alone can be slow. An expert teacher accelerates the pace, condenses the learning curve, and provides insights that could have been missed.

Teaching and learning are like a carefully choreographed dance. The teacher leads; the student responds. Teachers bring knowledge and skill to the dance, but the student brings an essential component—an intense desire to learn.

Moses was brilliant and educated in the courts of Egypt, but he recognized how much more he needed to learn.

"Now if I have indeed found favor in Your sight, please teach me Your ways, and I will know You and find favor in Your sight. Now consider that this nation is Your people." (Exod. 33:13)

King David was wise, but he knew he did not know enough to lead God's people.

Guide me in Your truth and teach me, for You are the God of my salvation; I wait for You all day long. (Ps. 25:5)

Having a great teacher does not guarantee that great learning will occur. Even with God as their teacher, the people of Israel refused to accept God's instruction.

They have turned their backs to Me and not their faces. Though I taught them time and time again, they do not listen and receive discipline. (Jer. 32:33)

We want to learn God's statutes and keep them, to understand His instruction, obey it, and follow it wholeheartedly. Pursuing these goals begins with a simple prayer, "Teach me, Lord."

Day 2

Pleasure

Help me stay on the path of Your commands, for I take pleasure in it. (Ps. 119:35)

People pursue pleasure in the wrong places. Fortunately, most people lack the funds to pursue pleasure in *all* the wrong places. One man, though, had the resources to indulge himself fully. His name was Solomon and he ran hard after the thrill—sex, creative pursuits, completing great projects. His unlimited riches enabled him to chase pleasure in all directions. After the race, he reflected on his experience and rendered an assessment.

I said to myself, "Go ahead, I will test you with pleasure; enjoy what is good." But it turned out to be futile. (Eccles. 2:1)

How odd that Solomon, one known for his wisdom, pursued a fool's path. Here's what distinguishes him: he was wise enough to recognize futility.

We find an example of a better choice with Moses. In spite of his privileges as a prince of Egypt, Moses set such pleasure aside. He traveled a different path, a difficult one. As a result, he was commended in the New Testament for his faith.

By faith Moses, when he had grown up, refused to be called the son of Pharaoh's daughter and chose to suffer with the people of God rather than to enjoy the short-lived pleasure of sin. (Heb. 11:24–25)

God has made it possible for us to experience pleasure in life, but doing so requires us to move down the path of His commands. God's Word explains how we can know God, be reconciled to Him, and how we can experience God working in our lives through His Holy Spirit. God's Word warns us of danger and points us to the things that will satisfy our souls.

As shameful conduct is pleasure for a fool, so wisdom is for a man of understanding. (Prov. 10:23)

We can learn from Solomon's futility. God has shown us the path of lasting pleasure.

Day 3

Turning

Turn my heart to Your decrees and not to material gain. Turn my eyes from looking at what is worthless; give me life in Your ways. (Ps. 119:36–37)

We have a turning problem. Left to our own inclinations, we turn to the wrong things. We fix our gaze on material gain and other things that are worthless. We turn wrongly, a flaw from the Fall of mankind in sin. Our turning mechanism broke, and only God can repair it.

The apostle Paul encountered Jesus on the road to Damascus. Recounting that experience in his testimony, Paul shared some of the things the resurrected Jesus said to him as He explained Paul's future mission.

"To open their eyes so they may turn from darkness to light and from the power of Satan to God, that by faith in Me they may receive forgiveness of sins and a share among those who are sanctified." (Acts 26:18)

The core of the gospel message centers on turning—turning to God in the way He has revealed in His Word and turning away from all else. This turning problem is not limited to a few. The sad truth is that none of us turn well on our own.

All have turned away; all alike have become corrupt. There is no one who does good, not even one. (Ps. 53:3)

On our own, we lack the desire or the capacity to turn. We need God to turn our hearts, to turn our eyes, and to give us life. Untethered from God, we drift predictably toward what is worthless. Tragically, there is abundant worthlessness on which to crash.

God's initial work in our hearts is to turn us to Him so that we can be saved. Having been given new life spiritually, we have a new capacity. We desire different things. Yes, the old enticements continue. Those who have feasted on the finest are still tempted inexplicably to dine from dumpsters. So we pray that the God who turned us initially from sin to Him will turn us continually from worthless things to life in His ways.

Day 4

Confirmation

Confirm what You said to Your servant, for it produces reverence for You. (Ps. 119:38)

God makes promises throughout the Bible. Some promises have been fulfilled; others, not yet. But every fulfilled promise bolsters the faith of those relying on promises yet to come.

One of God's great promises related to the exile of the people of Israel. After years of flaunting sin, God brought Babylon to Jerusalem. The foreign king destroyed the walls of the city, burned the temple and other buildings, and took the people as exiles to Babylon.

While the exiles waited to know God's plans, God spoke an astonishing promise through the prophet Jeremiah.

For this is what the LORD says: "When 70 years for Babylon are complete, I will attend to you and will confirm My promise concerning you to restore you to this place." (Jer. 29:10)

In time, that is exactly what happened. A new king allowed the people to return to their land and even financed the rebuilding of the temple and the walls. That fulfilled promise provided profound confirmation of God's sovereign power to accomplish what He proclaims.

After years of the Old Testament prophets foretelling the coming of God's Messiah, Jesus came and accomplished all that God had prescribed. After His death and resurrection, the disciples explained the significance of what had happened to the gathered crowd.

But what God predicted through the mouth of all the prophets—that His Messiah would suffer—He has fulfilled in this way. Therefore repent and turn back, so that your sins may be wiped out, that seasons of refreshing may come from the presence of the Lord. (Acts 3:18–19)

When the people heard this truth, they were struck with awe and reverence for God and wanted to know what to do. It's the same for us. When we read God's Word and see how He has fulfilled His promises for centuries, we bow in reverence to this great God.

Day 5

Disgrace

Turn away the disgrace I dread; indeed, Your judgments are good. How I long for Your precepts! Give me life through Your righteousness. (Ps. 119:39–40)

Some scholars believe King David wrote Psalm 119. That may be true. Other psalms attributed to David contain similar language. But if David did write this psalm, he did so before the tragedy of Bathsheba and her husband, Uriah.

The story is well known. Instead of going off to war, David stayed home. A furtive glance from his rooftop revealed a beautiful woman bathing. David inquired about her. The report should have stopped him cold.

So David sent someone to inquire about her, and he reported, "This is Bathsheba, daughter of Eliam and wife of Uriah the Hittite." (2 Sam. 11:3)

This beautiful woman was someone's daughter. She was married. And if that wasn't reason enough to stop David's headfirst plunge into disgrace, the next statement should have jerked him back. Bathsheba's husband was Uriah, one of David's Mighty Men, the group of valiant warriors who had risked their lives for years so that he could become king.

David was undeterred, and the tragedy progressed like a slow-motion crash. The disgrace was complete. The scandal became public. David, the man after God's own heart, would forever live with a footnote on his record of discipleship.

For David did what was right in the LORD's eyes, and he did not turn aside from anything He had commanded him all the days of his life, except in the matter of Uriah the Hittite. (1 Kings 15:5)

Disgrace is a true possibility and should be dreaded. Acknowledging God's good judgments and longing to live by His precepts protects us from a fall. Asking God to allow us to walk every day in His righteous path provides guardrails for our lives. Only a fool would not dread a fall. If David could fall, so can we. God's Word gives us ample reasons to remain vigilant.

Give Me Life in Your Ways
Psalm 119:33–40

Verse 1

Teach me, LORD, the meaning of Your statutes, and I'll always keep them.

Help me understand Your instruction, and I will obey it.

And follow it with all my heart.

Help me stay on the path of Your commands.

For I take pleasure in it.

Chorus

Turn my heart to Your decrees and not to material gain.

Turn my eyes from looking at what is worthless; give me life in Your ways.

Turn my heart; turn my eyes. Give me life in Your ways.

Verse 2

Confirm what You said to Your servant, for it produces reverence for You.

Turn away disgrace, the disgrace I dread.

Indeed, Your judgments, judgments are good.

How I long for Your precepts!

Give me life through Your righteousness.

Final Chorus

Turn my heart to Your decrees and not to material gain.

Turn my eyes from looking at what is worthless; give me life in Your ways.

Turn my heart; turn my eyes. Give me life in Your ways.

Turn my heart; turn my eyes. Give me life in Your ways.

Chapter 6

Never Take
the Word

Let Your faithful love come to me, LORD, Your salvation, as You promised.

Then I can answer the one who taunts me, for I trust in Your word.

Never take the word of truth from my mouth, for I hope in Your judgments.

I will always keep Your law, forever and ever.

I will walk freely in an open place because I seek Your precepts.

I will speak of Your decrees before kings and not be ashamed.

I delight in Your commands, which I love.

I will lift up my hands to Your commands, which I love, and will meditate on Your statutes.

—Psalm 119:41–48

Day 1

Love

Let Your faithful love come to me, LORD, Your salvation, as You promised. (Ps. 119:41)

God has revealed His love to us. On our own, we might have imagined a god and made up an image to worship. But we could never have imagined a god of love such as the true God. From the earliest days of His revelation, people have marveled at the reality of His love.

You will lead the people You have redeemed with Your faithful love; You will guide them to Your holy dwelling with Your strength. (Exod. 15:13)

One writer of psalms marveled at this God who loved His people.

But I enter Your house by the abundance of Your faithful love; I bow down toward Your holy temple in reverential awe of You. (Ps. 5:7)

When the people sinned, the prophets called them back to the God who loved.

Tear your hearts, not just your clothes, and return to the LORD your God. For He is gracious and compassionate, slow to anger, rich in faithful love, and He relents from sending disaster. (Joel 2:13)

The clearest picture, though, of God's faithful love was His plan for salvation. The Bible tells of one old saint, Simeon, who waited at the temple for years, yearning to see the one who would embody God's love for a lost world.

Simeon took Him up in his arms, praised God, and said: Now, Master, You can dismiss Your slave in peace, as You promised. For my eyes have seen Your salvation. (Luke 2:28–30)

God's faithful love came to us in human flesh, the means of salvation, the fulfillment of long–made promises. The implications of His coming were staggering then and arrest our wandering thoughts today. God came in time and opened a door to eternity. We can only marvel with Charles Wesley as he wrote, "Amazing love! How can it be, that Thou, my God, shouldst die for me?"

Day 2

Taunting

Then I can answer the one who taunts me, for I trust in Your word. (Ps. 119:42)

No one likes to be taunted. Big-mouthed bullies provoke with insulting remarks. Petty individuals clump together to become a jeering group, mocking and heaping sarcasm. They look with disdain on those different from them, scorning the things for which they stand.

Those who taunt find many targets, but one of their favorites is people of faith. They stand in a long line of the mean spirited.

My adversaries taunt me, as if crushing my bones, while all day long they say to me, "Where is your God?" (Ps. 42:10)

The children's rhyme about only sticks and stones breaking bones isn't true. Words hurt. Critics pound away, challenging the audacity of faith. For them it is a game from which they do not tire.

My enemies taunt me all day long; they ridicule and curse me. (Ps. 102:8)

The prophets encouraged the people of God not to give in to relentless taunts.

Listen to Me, you who know righteousness, the people in whose heart is My instruction: do not fear disgrace by men, and do not be shattered by their taunts. (Isa. 51:7)

We cannot allow their taunts to deter us from our opportunity to answer.

But even if you should suffer for righteousness, you are blessed. Do not fear what they fear or be disturbed, but honor the Messiah as Lord in your hearts. Always be ready to give a defense to anyone who asks you for a reason for the hope that is in you. (1 Pet. 3:14–15)

Often people mock what they do not understand. Our assignment is to trust in God's Word, absorb the taunts, and deflect their insulting words with kind answers of hope.

Day 3

Truth

Never take the word of truth from my mouth, for I hope in Your judgments. I will always keep Your law, forever and ever. (Ps. 119:43–44)

Once we grow accustomed to knowing God's Word and basing our lives on it, we cannot imagine no longer having it. Our experience with God is packaged in His Word, connecting and reflecting what He wants us to know and live out. Here's how Moses described God's Word to the people of Israel:

For they are not meaningless words to you but they are your life. (Deut. 32:47)

Our spiritual enemy hates the thought of us having God's Word, His seed, planted in our hearts. From the earliest stage of our experience with God, Satan works to keep that good seed from taking root in our hearts.

"This is the meaning of the parable: The seed is the word of God. The seed along the path are those who have heard and then the Devil comes and takes away the word from their hearts, so that they may not believe and be saved." (Luke 8:11–12)

We can know God's Word, but its power is blunted in us if we fail to align our lives to it.

Still, the LORD *warned Israel and Judah through every prophet and every seer, saying, "Turn from your evil ways and keep My commands and statutes according to all the law I commanded your ancestors and sent to you through My servants the prophets." (2 Kings 17:13)*

Because of God's gracious gift of His truth to us in His Word, we can know it and align our lives to it. Our intention is clear—to go God's way, reveling in His Word throughout this life and into eternity. Let there never be a time when God's truth is not in our mouths, this Word that will last forever and ever.

Day 4

Audience

I will walk freely in an open place because I seek Your precepts. I will speak of Your decrees before kings and not be ashamed. (Ps. 119:45–46)

Those entrusted with God's Word are commanded to speak publicly, and not just among our peers. Perhaps you'll tell God that public speaking is not your gift. Actually, Moses already tried that dodge to get out of a speaking assignment. It didn't work.

Yahweh said to him, "Who made the human mouth? Who makes him mute or deaf, seeing or blind? Is it not I, Yahweh? Now go! I will help you speak and I will teach you what to say." (Exod. 4:11–12)

As God directed, Moses did stand before Pharaoh and proclaim, "Thus says the Lord." Centuries later, the apostle Paul stood before a group of people in Corinth and told the good news of God. Mocked by some for his lack of speaking abilities, Paul reflected on his experience in Corinth.

I came to you in weakness, in fear, and in much trembling. My speech and my proclamation were not with persuasive words of wisdom but with a powerful demonstration by the Spirit, so that your faith might not be based on men's wisdom but on God's power. (1 Cor. 2:3–5)

Moses and Paul were extraordinary spiritual leaders. Perhaps, we speculate, God's power for public speaking is limited and does not apply to rank-and-file disciples. No way. Listen to what Jesus told His disciples.

"But when they hand you over, don't worry about how or what you should speak. For you will be given what to say at that hour, because you are not speaking, but the Spirit of your Father is speaking through you." (Matt. 10:19–20)

The moment God calls us to speak, His Spirit draws on God's truth that we have stored in our hearts. We will speak boldly and without shame. There may be others in the room, even rulers and kings. But we will speak for an audience of one—our King.

Day 5

Lifting

I delight in Your commands, which I love. I will lift up my hands to Your commands, which I love, and will meditate on Your statutes. (Ps. 119:47–48)

In times of joy and celebration, at a sporting event for example, people pop up their hands, waving and cheering. The action is spontaneous, natural.

Much of what God exhorts us to do with His Word requires internal responses. We delight in and love God's commands. We meditate on God's statutes. But is that the full range of response? Not for the psalmist.

So I will praise You as long as I live; at Your name, I will lift up my hands. (Ps. 63:4)

We can understand hands raised in joy, but what about during crushing experiences of sorrow? Surprisingly, we find a similar response.

I sought the Lord in my day of trouble. My hands were continually lifted up all night long; I refused to be comforted. (Ps. 77:2)

God's Word equips us for worship, not a fact-filled pop test. We need His commands and His statutes so that we can be prepared for times of exhilaration and excruciating loss. God gives us perspective on both joy and sorrow and the long roads between where we spend most of our lives.

Physical movements such as lifting hands cannot substitute for God's Word. They can, however, punctuate our experience with God's Word. God created us as multisensory beings, not just fact-processors. We have powerful emotions, strong wills, and bodies to express our complexity. So before the Lord, we celebrate our privilege of worshipping Him with all the tools He has given us, joining the psalmist in this declaration.

So I will praise You as long as I live; at Your name, I will lift up my hands. (Ps. 63:4)

Never Take the Word
Psalm 119:41–48

Verse 1

Let your faithful love come to me, LORD; Your salvation as you promised.

Then I can answer the one who taunts me; for I trust in Your Word.

Chorus

Never take the word of truth from my mouth.

For I hope in Your judgments.

I will always keep, always keep Your law;

keep Your law forever and ever.

Keep Your law forever and ever.

Verse 2

I will walk freely in an open place because I seek Your precepts.

I will speak of Your decrees before kings and not be ashamed.

Repeat Chorus

Bridge

I delight in Your commands, Your commands which I love.

I will lift, lift up my hands to Your commands which I love

And will meditate on Your statutes.

Repeat Chorus and Close

Never take the word of truth from my mouth. For I hope in Your judgments.

I will always keep always keep Your law; keep Your law forever and ever.

Keep Your law forever and ever.

Chapter 7

Your Statutes

Remember Your word to Your servant; You have given me hope through it.

This is my comfort in my affliction: Your promise has given me life.

The arrogant constantly ridicule me, but I do not turn away from Your instruction.

LORD, I remember Your judgments from long ago and find comfort.

Rage seizes me because of the wicked who reject Your instruction.

Your statutes are the theme of my song during my earthly life.

I remember Your name in the night, LORD, and I keep Your law.

This is my practice: I obey Your precepts.

—Psalm 119:49–56

Day 1

Remember

Remember Your word to Your servant; You have given me hope through it. This is my comfort in my affliction: Your promise has given me life. (Ps. 119:49–50)

Throughout the Old Testament God called His people to remember all He had done for them. Apparently, spiritual absentmindedness was epidemic. Sometimes, though, God's people grew concerned that He had forgotten about them. So they called out for God to remember.

So he is oppressed and beaten down; the helpless fall because of his strength. He says to himself, "God has forgotten; He hides His face and will never see." (Ps. 10:10–12)

God's words infuse us with hope for the future. But in the midst of trials, we can falter. The prophet Jeremiah represented God to the nation of Israel in a time of rebellion. Resenting God, they persecuted Jeremiah. He called out to God for help.

You know, LORD; remember me and take note of me. Avenge me against my persecutors. In Your patience, don't take me away. (Jer. 15:15)

In a similar way, the prophet Habakkuk struggled to see God's work in the midst of his troubles. He had heard of God's great work in the past, but he was no longer seeing it.

LORD, I have heard the report about You; Lord, I stand in awe of Your deeds. Revive Your work in these years; make it known in these years. In Your wrath remember mercy! (Hab. 3:2)

One of the Old Testament kings, Hezekiah, faced death from illness and called out to God.

Then Hezekiah turned his face to the wall and prayed to the LORD, "Please LORD, remember how I have walked before You faithfully and wholeheartedly and have done what pleases You." And Hezekiah wept bitterly. (2 Kings 20:2–3)

We trust God to remember us as He has promised. Circumstances will not trump His Word.

Day 2

Ago

The arrogant constantly ridicule me, but I do not turn away from Your instruction. LORD, I remember Your judgments from long ago and find comfort. (Ps. 119:51–52)

We live in a day of instant communication and information overload. Sadly, people place great value on what was written forty–seven seconds ago by someone they do not know and whose words they cannot validate. How much better to rely on God's Word, its instructions and judgments, written long ago and confirmed over centuries.

Remember what happened long ago, for I am God, and there is no other; I am God, and no one is like Me. I declare the end from the beginning, and from long ago what is not yet done, saying: My plan will take place, and I will do all My will. (Isa. 46:9–10)

God challenges the word producers of our day to a contest, the ultimate fact check. He lays down the gauntlet and says, in effect, "I declare the end from the beginning. Top that."

Speak up and present your case—yes, let them take counsel together. Who predicted this long ago? Who announced it from ancient times? Was it not I, Yahweh? There is no other God but Me, a righteous God and Savior; there is no one except Me. (Isa. 45:21)

Now we join those who have heard God's Word through the centuries, tested it, and discovered its veracity.

God, we have heard with our ears—our ancestors have told us—the work You accomplished in their days, in days long ago. (Ps. 44:1)

Let others ridicule us. Why would we turn from the greater to the lesser. So we stand with the long line of God's people who have found comfort in "Long Ago" words.

Yahweh, You are my God; I will exalt You. I will praise Your name, for You have accomplished wonders, plans formed long ago, with perfect faithfulness. (Isa. 25:1)

Forget what someone wrote forty–seven seconds ago. Stand on what God spoke before time.

Day 3

Rage

Rage seizes me because of the wicked who reject Your instruction. (Ps. 119:53)

From the beginning, people have reacted strongly to God. In spite of His power and love, they have arched their backs and gone their own way. Rather than submitting to God, men have built towers to honor themselves.

And they said, "Come, let us build ourselves a city and a tower with its top in the sky. Let us make a name for ourselves." (Gen. 11:4)

The prophet Isaiah spoke of the futility of raging against God.

The nations rage like the raging of many waters. He rebukes them, and they flee far away, driven before the wind like chaff on the hills and like tumbleweeds before a gale. (Isa. 17:13)

It is not just groups of people who resist God. Something in the individual fallen heart forcefully rejects God's Word.

A man's own foolishness leads him astray, yet his heart rages against the LORD. (Prov. 19:3)

Even when people encountered Jesus on earth, they responded violently, appalled that He would break the law and heal on the Sabbath.

They, however, were filled with rage and started discussing with one another what they might do to Jesus. (Luke 6:11)

It is natural for us to bristle with emotion when crass people mock God's Word. Rather than us picking the fight, we do well to let God deal with His opponents. He can defend His own reputation.

But I know your sitting down, your going out and your coming in, and your raging against Me. Because your raging against Me and your arrogance have reached My ears . . . I will make you go back the way you came. (2 Kings 19:27–28)

Day 4

Theme

Your statutes are the theme of my song during my earthly life. (Ps. 119:54)

If your life were a story, what would be its unifying idea? Or think of your life as a song with lyrics. What would be the "hook"? What would stand out and be most easily remembered? If your life were a piece of instrumental music, what would be the melodic subject? Perhaps you're thinking, *Who knew all this was so complicated!*

Whether we think about it or not, we establish a theme for our lives.

As the Israelites left Egypt and passed through the sea, they experienced God's power and extolled Him through music.

The LORD is my strength and my song; He has become my salvation. This is my God, and I will praise Him, my father's God, and I will exalt Him. (Exod. 15:2)

Later, King David would profess that God was the central focus of his life.

The LORD is my strength and my shield; my heart trusts in Him, and I am helped. Therefore my heart rejoices, and I praise Him with my song. (Ps. 28:7)

Without a unifying force, a dominating focus, our lives spin aimlessly. But with God's Word driving us back to a powerful relationship with the God of creation, we can find our theme. Actually, our theme can find us. The Bible includes countless stories of people who lived with God–themes while others settled for elevator music.

As a musician, King David knew the power of songs and made music a central part of his relationship with God.

The LORD will send His faithful love by day; His song will be with me in the night—a prayer to the God of my life. (Ps. 42:8)

Our earthly lives are short. Let's live them with the one worthy theme—God and His Word.

Day 5

Practice

I remember Your name in the night, LORD, and I keep Your law. This is my practice: I obey Your precepts. (Ps. 119:55–56)

"Practice makes perfect," so we are told. For something in our lives to become habitual, customary, and the established pattern, we must practice. We must do it over and over. While it is true that "practice makes perfect," what we practice can be far from perfect. As fallen people, we can be drawn to terrible things and begin to practice them.

They became callous and gave themselves over to promiscuity for the practice of every kind of impurity with a desire for more and more. (Eph. 4:19)

The consistent message of the Bible is that we must carefully practice the right things and consistently avoid practicing the wrong things. Here's the admonition Moses gave the Israelites.

Do not follow the practices of the land of Egypt, where you used to live, or follow the practices of the land of Canaan, where I am bringing you. You must not follow their customs.

You are to practice My ordinances and you are to keep My statutes by following them; I am Yahweh your God. (Lev. 18:3–4)

So what shapes our practices? By maintaining a continual focus on God's Word with its laws and precepts to help us understand God, we can grow closer to Him so He can intensify His transforming work in our hearts.

Do not lie to one another, since you have put off the old self with its practices and have put on the new self. You are being renewed in knowledge according to the image of your Creator. (Col. 3:9–10)

Our practice as Christians does not depend on our willpower. God's laws convinced us that we could not keep them, so we turned by faith to Christ. Now He works within us to give us new desires and power. In the end, only God's practice makes us perfect in Christ.

Your Statutes
Psalm 119:49–56

Verse 1

Remember Your word, Your word to Your servant. You've given me hope through it.

This is my comfort in my affliction. Your promise has given me life. Given me life.

Chorus

Your statutes are the theme of my song during my earthly life.

I remember Your name in the night, LORD, and I keep Your law.

This is my practice: I obey Your precepts.

Your statutes are the theme of my song during my earthly life.

Verse 2

The arrogant constantly ridicule me, but I do not turn away

From your instruction, LORD, I remember Your promise from long ago. Long ago.

Repeat Chorus

Bridge

Lord, I remember Your judgments from long ago and find comfort.

Rage seizes me because of the wicked who reject Your instruction.

Repeat Chorus and Close

Your statutes are the theme of my song during my earthly life.

I remember Your name in the night, LORD, and I keep Your law.

This is my practice: I obey Your precepts.

Your statutes are the theme of my song during my earthly life.

Your statutes are the theme of my song during my earthly life.

Chapter 8

Hurried, Not Hesitating

The LORD *is my portion; I have promised to keep Your words.*

I have sought Your favor with all my heart; be gracious to me according to Your promise.

I thought about my ways and turned my steps back to Your decrees.

I hurried, not hesitating to keep Your commands.

Though the ropes of the wicked were wrapped around me, I did not forget Your law.

I rise at midnight to thank You for Your righteous judgments.

I am a friend to all who fear You, to those who keep Your precepts.

LORD, *the earth is filled with Your faithful love; teach me Your statutes.*

—Psalm 119:57–64

Day 1 ·

Portion

The LORD is my portion. (Ps. 119:57)

As the people of Israel prepared to conquer the Promised Land, Moses promised that each tribe would receive a portion of the land, with one exception—the tribe of Levi.

For this reason, Levi does not have a portion or inheritance like his brothers; the LORD is his inheritance, as the LORD your God told him. (Deut. 10:9)

Rather than receiving land, the "portion" for the Levites was the privilege of leading the nation in worship and caring for the House of the Lord. Land to eleven tribes; the Lord to one tribe. Which received the greater portion?

Years later, King David reflected on His relationship with God using this analogy.

I cry to You, LORD; I say, "You are my shelter, my portion in the land of the living." (Ps. 142:5)

How valuable is it to have the Lord as our portion today? We must look past the temporal to the eternal. What is the value of a portion of the infinite?

The Bible tells of two brothers, Jacob and Esau. Once when Esau returned from hunting, he was famished and wanted the stew his brother was cooking. Jacob offered to trade stew for Esau's birthright, his position of spiritual privilege as the firstborn.

"Look," said Esau, "I'm about to die, so what good is a birthright to me?" Jacob said, "Swear to me first." So he swore to Jacob and sold his birthright to him. Then Jacob gave bread and lentil stew to Esau; he ate, drank, got up,

and went away. So Esau despised his birthright. (Gen. 25:32–34)

In life, we trade pennies for treasure or treasure for pennies. Our relationship with God through Jesus Christ is our spiritual portion, the ultimate treasure. So what is the value of what we have received? The cross was the price of our portion, so whatever we give in exchange is a bargain. Our lives—pennies; His life—treasure. The choice is clear.

Day 2

Favor

I have sought Your favor with all my heart; be gracious to me according to Your promise. (Ps. 119:58)

Being in a right relationship with God is the apex of life. Without salvation, nothing else matters. Once saved, we seek to live lives with God's favor—His approval, His support. We cannot earn God's favor any more than we can earn our salvation. God has revealed in His word the actions, decisions, and manner of life He will bless. If we seek truth in God's Word and allow God to align our lives to His revelation, we can pray for God's favor with confidence. We see the pattern throughout the Bible.

Noah, however, found favor in the sight of the LORD. (Gen. 6:8)

Then he said, "My lord, if I [Abraham] have found favor in your sight, please do not go on past your servant. (Gen. 18:3)

The LORD gave the people favor in the sight of the Egyptians. And the man Moses was highly regarded in the land of Egypt by Pharaoh's officials and the people. (Exod. 11:3)

By contrast, the boy Samuel grew in stature and in favor with the LORD and with men. (1 Sam. 2:26)

God had granted Daniel favor and compassion from the chief official. (Dan. 1:9)

Then the angel told her: Do not be afraid, Mary, for you have found favor with God. (Luke 1:30)

The ultimate example of living with the favor of God is Jesus during His earthly ministry.

And Jesus increased in wisdom and stature, and in favor with God and with people. (Luke 2:52)

Never because of merit, only based on grace, can we seek God's favor. Living life in the shelter of God's favor is an unspeakable privilege, one worth seeking with full hearts.

Day 3

Hurry

I thought about my ways and turned my steps back to Your decrees. I hurried, not hesitating to keep Your commands. (Ps. 119:59–60)

"Would you hurry up?"

It's a statement we make when someone moves at an inappropriate pace. Of course, we determine the correct pace and calculate the increased rate required. We issue "hurry ups" to other people regularly. We even try to hurry God. King David sometimes urged God to move more quickly.

I am afflicted and needy; hurry to me, God. You are my help and my deliverer; LORD, do not delay. (Ps. 70:5)

God, do not be far from me; my God, hurry to help me. (Ps. 71:12)

LORD, I call on You; hurry to help me. Listen to my voice when I call on You. (Ps. 141:1)

It's easy to spot others moving too slowly, but it's harder to pace our lives spiritually. How quickly do we move when we see gaps in our lives compared to God's commands? If we're not careful, we can become like the people in the days of the prophet Elijah.

So Ahab summoned all the Israelites and gathered the prophets at Mount Carmel. Then Elijah approached all the people and said, "How long will you hesitate between two opinions? If Yahweh is God, follow Him. But if Baal, follow him." But the people didn't answer him a word. (1 Kings 18:20–21)

We want to live with God's favor. Well, God favors those who monitor and close spiritual gaps that form in their lives. At the first sign of a gap, warning lights flash. They act. No hesitating, no dangling between two opinions. Delayed obedience is disobedience. They confess, repent, and ask for strength to get back on track.

It's exhausting to hurry other people. Forget about it. Instead, ask God to help you to hurry and not hesitate to obey Him.

Day 4

Tangled

Though the ropes of the wicked were wrapped around me, I did not forget Your law. I rise at midnight to thank You for Your righteous judgments. (Ps. 119:61–62)

It's disheartening to realize that some people delight in your downfall. In fact, they try to trip you. Their actions are wicked, and God will judge them. But what can you do now to avoid a fall? You have only one hope.

Protect me, LORD, from the clutches of the wicked. Keep me safe from violent men who plan to make me stumble. The proud hide a trap with ropes for me; they spread a net along the path and set snares for me. (Ps. 140:4–5)

Even if you try, you cannot protect yourself completely from the wicked. Your focus on God's law and all of His Word will enhance your spiritual preparation. In the end, God must protect you from the traps enemies set.

The LORD is righteous; He has cut the ropes of the wicked. (Ps. 129:4)

Samson, one of Israel's judges, became entangled with a prostitute, Delilah. In the past, God had always helped him escape, so Samson gave his enemies multiple chances to trap him.

Then she let him fall asleep on her lap and called a man to shave off the seven braids on his head. In this way, she made him helpless, and his strength left him. Then she cried, "Samson, the Philistines are here!" When he awoke from his sleep, he said, "I will escape as I did before and shake myself free." But he did not know that the LORD had left him. (Judg. 16:19–20)

Samson's story did not have to end that way. He should have been at home, rising at midnight and thanking God for His righteous judgments. Instead, he presumed on God's grace and became tangled in sin. There are people who will laugh if you fall. So why make it easier for them? If you can see their laps, you're recklessly close. Run.

Day 5

All

I am a friend to all who fear You, to those who keep Your precepts. LORD, the earth is filled with Your faithful love; teach me Your statutes. (Ps. 119:63–64)

Millions have turned to God through Jesus Christ and locked arms in fellowship. Together, we stand as those who fear the Lord, who acknowledge His mighty power, and bow before Him in reverent awe. We marvel at His faithful love and long to learn more of His truth. Our hearts resonate with the words of the apostle John:

If we say, "We have fellowship with Him," yet we walk in darkness, we are lying and are not practicing the truth. But if we walk in the light as He Himself is in the light, we have fellowship with one another, and the blood of Jesus His Son cleanses us from all sin. (1 John 1:6–7)

What a circle we form in Christ, we who seek the Lord and take refuge in Him.

Let all who seek You rejoice and be glad in You; let those who love Your salvation continually say, "The LORD is great!" (Ps. 40:16)

But let all who take refuge in You rejoice; let them shout for joy forever. May You shelter them, and may those who love Your name boast about You. (Ps. 5:11)

The company of Christ is our circle of eternal friends. We hold in our hearts those we have never met but who know Christ. We commit them to the Lord and pray for His transforming work in their lives, the same work He is doing in us. In this, we stand in the great tradition of the beginning days of the church.

"And now I commit you to God and to the message of His grace, which is able to build you up and to give you an inheritance among all who are sanctified." (Acts 20:32)

All who confess that Jesus is Lord are bound to us. Much separates us—language and culture—but stronger bonds connect us all.

Hurried, Not Hesitating
Psalm 119:57–64

Verse 1

The LORD is my portion; I have promised
To keep Your words, I've promised to keep Your words.
I've sought Your favor with all my heart;
be gracious to me according to Your promise.

Chorus

I thought about my ways and turned my steps,
Turned my steps back to Your decrees.
I hurried, not hesitating to keep Your commands.
I hurried, not hesitating to keep Your commands.

Verse 2

Though the ropes of the wicked
were wrapped around me, I did not forget Your law.
I rise at midnight, at midnight to thank You
for Your righteous, for Your righteous judgments.

Repeat Chorus

Bridge

I am a friend to all who fear You, to those who keep
Your precepts.
Lord, the earth is filled with Your faithful love, with
Your faithful love.
Teach me Your statutes.

Repeat Chorus and Close

I thought about my ways and turned my steps,
Turned my steps back to Your decrees.
I hurried, not hesitating to keep Your commands.
I hurried, not hesitating to keep Your commands.

Chapter 9

You're Good

LORD, You have treated Your servant well, just as You promised.

Teach me good judgment and discernment, for I rely on Your commands.

Before I was afflicted I went astray, but now I keep Your word.

You are good, and You do what is good; teach me Your statutes.

The arrogant have smeared me with lies, but I obey Your precepts with all my heart.

Their hearts are hard and insensitive, but I delight in Your instruction.

It was good for me to be afflicted so that I could learn Your statutes.

Instruction from Your lips is better for me than thousands of gold and silver pieces.

—Psalm 119:65–72

Day 1

Treated

LORD, *You have treated Your servant well, just as You promised. Teach me good judgment and discernment, for I rely on Your commands. (Ps. 119:65–66)*

How do you expect to be treated? It's an important question that reveals much about our spiritual discernment. Jesus pointed out this paradox.

Woe to you when all people speak well of you, for this is the way their ancestors used to treat the false prophets. (Luke 6:26)

In contrast, when Jesus talked about His life on earth, He had different expectations.

"How then is it written about the Son of Man that He must suffer many things and be treated with contempt?" (Mark 9:12)

In the same way, the testimony of the apostle Paul and others in the early church was that they were treated harshly most of the time.

Up to the present hour we are both hungry and thirsty; we are poorly clothed, roughly treated. (1 Cor. 4:11)

Proper expectations for our treatment require spiritual judgment and discernment. Such insight begins with God's promises filtered through God's commands.

Unless we are careful, we will value too little how God has treated us and fixate on the treatment of others. Once we understand the magnitude of our sin and the hopelessness of our standing before God, we glimpse God's incredible graciousness to us in Christ. We deserved eternal punishment. He treated us with ultimate mercy.

Our testimony is emphatic: "God, You've treated us well." We calibrate all other expectations from that starting point. When others treat us poorly because we follow Christ, why would we be surprised? They crucified Jesus. Should we expect white gloves and party manners when they deal with us?

Day 2

Afflicted

Before I was afflicted I went astray, but now I keep Your word. . . . It was good for me to be afflicted so that I could learn Your statutes. (Ps. 119:67, 71)

We have affirmed that God has treated us well in Christ. But what if He sovereignly allows pain, suffering, and distress to come to our lives? Would we still praise Him? Could we acknowledge a positive purpose for affliction?

Sin flawed the human race at a fundamental level we cannot grasp. As a result, our impulses are off. Things that should be good can have bad effects. We all want to have happy, healthy, and prosperous lives. But what if some or all of those perceived benefits cause us to move away from God? Moses warned the Israelites about this problem:

You may say to yourself, "My power and my own ability have gained this wealth for me," but remember that the LORD your God gives you the power to gain wealth, in order to confirm His covenant He swore to your fathers, as it is today. If you ever forget the LORD your God and go after other gods to worship and bow down to them, I testify against you today that you will perish. (Deut. 8:17–19)

The entire book of Judges describes the Israelites' recurring pattern: they prospered, they abandoned God, they experienced affliction, God rescued them, things got better until they pushed the repeat button and the sorry cycle began again.

What if affliction radically increased your knowledge of God's Word? What if pain, suffering, and distress made it possible for you to learn about and obey God in ways that would not have been possible in any other way? So should you pray for God to afflict you? No. We don't have to seek affliction; it's packaged with life. The question is how we will think about it. As God gives us grace and as we walk with Him, we can say, "It was good for me to be afflicted." That's a statement only God can empower us to make and mean it.

Day 3

Good

You are good, and You do what is good; teach me Your statutes. (Ps. 119:68)

Nothing challenges our view of God like affliction. If God is good, why does He allow bad things to happen to us? If God is all-powerful, why doesn't He stop our affliction? The writer of this psalm grappled with this perplexing problem.

"God, you are good." The Bible reveals God's holiness, His absolute purity.

"God, you do what is good." The Bible explains that a holy and pure God does only good actions.

The Bible confirms these twin affirmations. Anything in life we perceive as good reflects the intrinsic goodness of God. Where would we get the idea of "good" or "perfect" if God did not exist to provide the objective standard?

Making these confessions and living them out in the suffering of life is challenging. When we become disoriented, we must stop and consider the worst day in human history, the day wicked people murdered Jesus. The Bible explains how a good and all-powerful God did what was good that day—foreknowing, predestining, calling, justifying, and glorifying.

We know that all things work together for the good of those who love God: those who are called according to His purpose. For those He foreknew He also predestined to be conformed to the image of His Son, so that He would be the firstborn among many brothers. And those He predestined, He also called; and those He called, He also justified; and those He justified, He also glorified. (Rom. 8:28–30)

We must learn God's statutes so we will never trivialize afflictions with platitudes. By faith, we rest, confident that God works through pain and suffering to accomplish good purposes. The "good" may not yet be clear, but the ultimate outcome is sure.

Day 4

Smeared

The arrogant have smeared me with lies, but I obey Your precepts with all my heart. Their hearts are hard and insensitive, but I delight in Your instruction. (Ps. 119:69–70)

Affliction has many faces, one of which is lies. If you set your heart to know and obey God's Word, your enemies will lie about you. They will invent tales of what you have said or done, coating you with gross, greasy, sticky stories, hoping that at least a few will stick.

Lying is foul work done by those with an exaggerated sense of self-importance. Their arrogance makes it easier for them to inflict pain on you without remorse.

Because of the darkness in their own souls, liars detest those who strive to follow God's Word. Your obedience to God's precepts provokes them; your delight in God's instruction mocks them. They see God's Word in you and feel small, so they belittle you. Bringing you down is the only way they can increase in their own eyes.

The pain their lies inflict on you does not bother them. Long before they started smearing you with lies, they slathered self-justifying protection on their hearts. Telling themselves lies made it easier to lie about you. Hardened hearts lie better.

So how do you protect yourself? Don't engage them; doing so only confirms they have cut you. Defend yourself publicly and they will twist your statements. Your best option is to wait, allowing the truth to refute their lies.

Like a flitting sparrow or a fluttering swallow, an undeserved curse goes nowhere. (Prov. 26:2)

Even a mountain of lies cannot bury the truth of God's Word. Keep obeying; continue delighting. Fix your eyes on Jesus, the way, the truth, and the life.

I have not written to you because you don't know the truth, but because you do know it, and because no lie comes from the truth. (1 John 2:21)

Day 5

Better

Instruction from Your lips is better for me than thousands of gold and silver pieces. (Ps. 119:72)

Give us two options and we presume we can choose the better one. Of course we can determine which is more useful, suitable, or desirable. Never do we consider that our perception may be flawed. But it is. As a consequence of the Fall, our filters fail. We strain out the better options and settle for lesser ones. The cumulative impact of bad choices crushes us. We desperately need a better "better" filter.

Sure, we don't make the worst choice every time. If the contrast is stark, such as a decision between a diamond and an orange peel, we may chose the diamond . . . at least two out of three times. But when the differences are subtle, a temporal diamond for an eternal vault of treasure, our faulty filters go haywire. Unaided, we consistently make wrong choices on the ultimate matters in life.

We must have God's Word, objective truth, so we can discern what is better and choose it. Rather than becoming distracted by a con man's shell game, God helps us recognize the glint of true valuables. The Bible reveals what is better.

The little that the righteous man has is better than the abundance of many wicked people. (Ps. 37:16)

My lips will glorify You because Your faithful love is better than life. (Ps. 63:3)

Better a day in Your courts than a thousand anywhere else. (Ps. 84:10)

God's Word points us to God, the way of salvation through Jesus Christ.

Even though we are speaking this way, dear friends, in your case we are confident of the better things connected with salvation. (Heb. 6:9)

Knowing Jesus is infinitely better than anything in this world. God opens our eyes to see what is better. Having discerned the difference, we purpose to pursue "better" and never look back.

You're Good
Psalm 119:65–72

Opening Chorus

You're good and You do what's good. You're good and You do what's good.

Do what is good; teach me Your statutes.

Verse 1

The arrogant have smeared me with lies, but I obey Your precepts with all my heart.

Their hearts are hard and insensitive, but I delight, delight in Your instruction.

Chorus

LORD, You've treated Your servant well, just as You promised.

Teach me good judgment, discernment, for I rely on Your commands.

Before I was afflicted I went astray, but now I keep Your word.

You're good and You do what's good. You're good and You do what's good.

Do what is good; teach me Your statutes.

Verse 2

It was good for me to be afflicted so, so that I could learn, could learn Your statutes.

Instruction from Your lips is better for me than thousands of gold and silver pieces.

Repeat Chorus

Bridge

Instruction from Your lips is better for me than thousands of gold and silver pieces.

Better for me, so much better for me than thousands of gold and silver pieces.

Final Chorus

Before I was afflicted I went astray, but now I keep Your word.

You're good and You do what's good. You're good and You do what's good.

Do what is good; teach me Your statutes.

Chapter 10

Faithful Love

Your hands made me and formed me; give me understanding so that I can learn Your commands.

Those who fear You will see me and rejoice, for I put my hope in Your word.

I know, LORD, that Your judgments are just and that You have afflicted me fairly.

May Your faithful love comfort me, as You promised Your servant.

May Your compassion come to me so that I may live, for Your instruction is my delight.

Let the arrogant be put to shame for slandering me with lies; I will meditate on Your precepts.

Let those who fear You, those who know Your decrees, turn to me.

May my heart be blameless regarding Your statutes so that I will not be put to shame.

—Psalm 119:73–80

Day 1

Formed

Your hands made me and formed me; give me understanding so that I can learn Your commands. (Ps. 119:73)

Our perspective changes when we discover that God formed us. He brought our parts together and shaped us into unique people. The Bible speaks of this glorious mystery.

For it was You who created my inward parts; You knit me together in my mother's womb. I will praise You because I have been remarkably and wonderfully made. Your works are wonderful, and I know this very well. My bones were not hidden from You when I was made in secret, when I was formed in the depths of the earth. Your eyes saw me when I was formless; all my days were written in Your book and planned before a single one of them began. (Ps. 139:13–16)

God formed us personally. He created the first man from dust and formed mankind for His purpose and praise.

The people I formed for Myself will declare My praise. (Isa. 43:21)

God did not create us, wind us up, and leave us to run through life on our own. He remains mindful of His creation, monitoring and directing the course of our lives.

The LORD looks down from heaven; He observes everyone. He gazes on all the inhabitants of the earth from His dwelling place. He alone shapes their hearts; He considers all their works. (Ps. 33:13–15)

God's plan culminated in Christ, making it possible for our lives to be transformed into the image of His Son. The apostle Paul wrote of this process to one of the early churches.

My children, I am again suffering labor pains for you until Christ is formed in you. (Gal. 4:19)

Knowing that God created and formed us prompts us to seek understanding, learning His commands from His Word so that we accomplish the purposes for which we were created.

Day 2

Fairly

Those who fear You will see me and rejoice, for I put my hope in Your word. I know, LORD, that Your judgments are just and that You have afflicted me fairly. (Ps. 119:74–75)

Early on, children say, "That's not fair." The moral gyroscopes in their self-centered worlds tip, and they perceive they are getting less than what they deserve. For the world to be fair, they must get more. If things become unbalanced, they believe someone should take from others and give to them. That, of course, would be fair.

Those who know God's Word shudder at the thought of saying, "That's not fair." The last thing we want is for God to do for us what is fair. We don't want what we deserve; we plead for what we do not deserve—mercy.

I cry aloud to the LORD; I plead aloud to the LORD for mercy. (Ps. 142:1)

Mercy is our only option because of the perfect justice of God.

Your name, God, like Your praise, reaches to the ends of the earth; Your right hand is filled with justice. (Ps. 48:10)

God's Word reveals His unflinching justice but points to His provision for mercy.

But God, who is rich in mercy, because of His great love that He had for us, made us alive with the Messiah even though we were dead in trespasses. You are saved by grace! (Eph. 2:4–5)

We bow in awestruck reverence before God, putting our hope in Jesus and acknowledging that any judgment would be fair in light of our sin.

Because of the LORD's faithful love we do not perish, for His mercies never end. They are new every morning; great is Your faithfulness! (Lam. 3:22–23)

No matter what we experience in life, the only thing that is not fair is that Jesus died for our sins so that we could receive the mercy of God.

Day 3

Compassion

May Your faithful love comfort me, as You promised Your servant. May Your compassion come to me so that I may live, for Your instruction is my delight. (Ps. 119:76–77)

As Christians, we serve a God of compassion. He sympathizes with our concerns and misfortunes. He is deeply aware of our suffering and takes action to relieve it. Without God's compassion, we could not survive the crushing burdens of life.

As a father has compassion on his children, so the LORD has compassion on those who fear Him. (Ps. 103:13)

LORD, *do not withhold Your compassion from me; Your constant love and truth will always guard me. (Ps. 40:11)*

Within the context of God's promises, we experience God's faithful love and comfort. Reflecting on years of Israel's history, Nehemiah marveled at God's patient compassion:

You were patient with them for many years, and Your Spirit warned them through Your prophets, but they would not listen. Therefore, You handed them over to the surrounding peoples. However, in Your abundant compassion, You did not destroy them or abandon them, for You are a gracious and compassionate God. (Neh. 9:30–31)

Although forgiven of sin in Christ, we still stumble. Even then, God comforts us as we delight in His instruction and return to the way He has told us to walk.

He will again have compassion on us; He will vanquish our iniquities. You will cast all our sins into the depths of the sea. (Mic. 7:19)

God's faithful love comforts; His compassion comes to us. And so we testify:

I will make known the LORD's faithful love and the LORD's praiseworthy acts, because of all the LORD has done for us—even the many good things He has done for the house of Israel and has done for them based on His compassions and the abundance of His faithful love. (Isa. 63:7)

Day 4

Knowing

Let the arrogant be put to shame for slandering me with lies;
I will meditate on Your precepts. Let those who fear You,
those who know Your decrees, turn to me. (Ps. 119:78–79)

The Bible uses the word "knowing" differently than we do today. To know something or someone implied deep, intimate knowledge, insight, and understanding. The standard for "knowing" is the way the Bible reveals that God knows us.

LORD, You have searched me and known me. (Ps. 139:1)

Our knowledge is limited. We cannot know God as He knows us. Yet in Christ, He has given us spiritual eyes to grasp the mysteries of His ways, His work, and His will. God can give us increasingly sharp spiritual vision for which the apostle Paul prayed.

I pray that the perception of your mind may be enlightened
so you may know what is the hope of His calling, what are
the glorious riches of His inheritance among the saints, and
what is the immeasurable greatness of His power to us who
believe, according to the working of His vast strength. (Eph.
1:18–19)

The lies of the arrogant stand in stark contrast to the truth of God. That's why we turn from them and meditate on God's precepts. All who fear the Lord seek to know His decrees so that they may know Him more intimately. We acknowledge the gap between God and us.

Oh, the depth of the riches both of the wisdom and the
knowledge of God! How unsearchable His judgments and
untraceable His ways! For who has known the mind of the
Lord? Or who has been His counselor? (Rom. 11:33–34)

We know in part now. One day, perfect knowledge will swallow the incomplete.

For now we see indistinctly, as in a mirror, but then face to face. Now I know in part, but then I will know fully, as I am fully known. (1 Cor. 13:12)

We rally with those seeking to know God. One day we will know Him fully.

Day 5

Heart

May my heart be blameless regarding Your statutes so that I will not be put to shame. (Ps. 119:80)

If we desire blameless hearts, we face some daunting challenges. For one, our hearts lie to us. This is what the prophet Jeremiah discovered.

The heart is more deceitful than anything else, and incurable—who can understand it? (Jer. 17:9)

God's statutes reveal God's plumb line. In the same way a builder drops a string on a weight to determine if a wall is straight, God's Word provides the perfect standard to enable us to see the state of our hearts.

You have tested my heart; You have examined me at night. You have tried me and found nothing evil; I have determined that my mouth will not sin. (Ps. 17:3)

When God evaluates our hearts and reveals His findings, we face the depth of our spiritual heart disease. We cannot fix our old hearts; we need new hearts.

And I will give them one heart and put a new spirit within them; I will remove their heart of stone from their bodies and give them a heart of flesh. (Ezek. 11:19)

We face great pain in life if we deviate from God's statutes. Sin brings its own consequences, including the shame of having our sin discovered and broadcast. Our greater need, though, is to have hearts that are blameless before God.

May He make your hearts blameless in holiness before our God and Father at the coming of our Lord Jesus with all His saints. (1 Thess. 3:13)

For this reason, the Bible exhorts us to guard our hearts as a top priority.

Guard your heart above all else, for it is the source of life. (Prov. 4:23)

Our desperate problem was a bad heart. God's gracious gift to us was a new heart.

Faithful Love
Psalm 119:73–80

Verse 1

Your hands made me and formed me;
give me understanding so that I can learn Your commands.
Those who fear You will see me and rejoice, for I put my
hope in Your word.
I know, LORD, Your judgments are just and that You've
afflicted me fairly.

Chorus

May Your faithful love comfort me as You promised Your servant.

May Your compassion come to me so that I may live, for Your instruction is my delight, my delight.

May Your faithful love comfort me; may Your faithful love comfort me.

Verse 2

Let the arrogant be put to shame
for slandering me with lies.

I will meditate on Your precepts. Let those who fear You turn to me.

Let those who fear You, those who know Your decrees turn to me.

Repeat Chorus

Bridge

May my heart be blameless regarding Your statutes
so that I will not be put to shame.

Final Chorus and Close

May Your faithful love comfort me, as You promised Your servant.

May Your compassion come to me so that I may live,
for Your instruction is my delight, my delight.

May Your faithful love comfort me;
may Your faithful love comfort me.

Chapter 11

How Many Days

I long for Your salvation; I put my hope in Your word.

My eyes grow weary looking for what You have promised; I ask, "When will You comfort me?"

Though I have become like a wineskin dried by smoke, I do not forget Your statutes.

How many days must Your servant wait? When will You execute judgment on my persecutors?

The arrogant have dug pits for me; they violate Your instruction.

All Your commands are true; people persecute me with lies—help me!

They almost ended my life on earth, but I did not abandon Your precepts.

Give me life in accordance with Your faithful love, and I will obey the decree You have spoken.

—Psalm 119:81–88

Day 1

Focus

I long for Your salvation; I put my hope in Your word. My eyes grow weary looking for what You have promised; I ask, "When will You comfort me?" (Ps. 119:81–82)

Our lives with God are lives of focus. As His servants, we fix our eyes on Him.

I lift my eyes to You, the One enthroned in heaven. Like a servant's eyes on His master's hand, like a servant girl's eyes on her mistress's hand, so our eyes are on the LORD our God until He shows us favor. (Ps. 123:1–2)

Our salvation comes only from the Lord. Our hope comes only from God's Word. Our faith comes only in the context of God's promises. Where else can we look but Him? Often as we look to the Lord, we find immediate relief.

The precepts of the LORD are right, making the heart glad; the command of the LORD is radiant, making the eyes light up. (Ps. 19:8)

But not always. Other times we look to the Lord and feel confused. We wait for relief and see only more difficulties heading our way. King David shared that experience.

I am weary from my crying; my throat is parched. My eyes fail, looking for my God. (Ps. 69:3)

In his suffering, Job searched desperately and could find no relief.

My eyes have grown dim from grief, and my whole body has become but a shadow. (Job 17:7)

A determined focus on God's Word does not alleviate struggle. If anything, knowing God's Word prepares us not to see answers immediately. As a result, we can maintain a steady focus on God when we see nothing else, no clear answers to prayer, no relief from suffering. Failing to see God's actions frees us to focus only on Him. Sometimes our greatest comfort is focusing on the truth about God in His Word even when we feel no evidence of that truth. We can focus in spite of how we feel, trusting that God works even when we cannot see evidence of His activities.

Day 2

Preparation

Though I have become like a wineskin dried by smoke, I do not forget Your statutes. (Ps. 119:83)

Everyone in Jesus' day knew about wineskins, so He referred to them in His teaching.

"And no one puts new wine into old wineskins. Otherwise, the skins burst, the wine spills out, and the skins are ruined. But they put new wine into fresh wineskins, and both are preserved." (Matt. 9:17)

Curing skins with smoke made them flexible and able to store wine, water, or other things. In the same way, God equips, molds, and shapes us. He matches the intensity and duration of our preparation to the nature of our assignment. Sometimes we can discern the contours of God's future plans for us by the force of the current pressures on our lives.

Simon Peter became one of the strongest leaders in the early church but only after crushing preparation. Jesus gave him advanced warning.

"Simon, Simon, look out! Satan has asked to sift you like wheat. But I have prayed for you that your faith may not fail. And you, when you have turned back, strengthen your brothers." (Luke 22:31–32)

The spiritual sifting served a good purpose. Given the option, Simon Peter would have skipped that difficult night, but all that happened was required for a positive outcome.

We also struggle with the troubles in life; they are irritating and debilitating. While waiting in the spiritual smokehouse, we can reflect on God's Word.

So if anyone purifies himself from anything dishonorable, he will be a special instrument, set apart, useful to the Master, prepared for every good work. (2 Tim. 2:21)

We can be confident that God will not waste the smoke in our lives. He will use only what is required for us to function as His special instruments.

Day 3

Counting

How many days must Your servant wait? When will You execute judgment on my persecutors? (Ps. 119:84)

Often the spiritual smoke God uses to prepare our lives is other people. The crushing we feel comes from people we can see. Why, we wonder, does God delay in dealing with them? Why not judge them now?

For years while Saul was king of Israel, he hunted David, seeking to kill him to protect the throne. Tragically insecure, Saul worried that David would steal the kingdom. Saul totally misunderstood the plans of God and discounted the character of David. Even when he had the opportunity to kill Saul, David refused to do so.

> "May the LORD judge between you and me, and may the LORD take vengeance on you for me, but my hand will never be against you. As the old proverb says, 'Wickedness comes from wicked people.' My hand will never be against you." (1 Sam. 24:12–13)

David believed that God would vindicate him against Saul. That did not mean, however, that David did not grow weary waiting for God to act.

> David said to himself, "One of these days I'll be swept away by Saul. There is nothing better for me than to escape immediately to the land of the Philistines. Then Saul will stop searching for me everywhere in Israel, and I'll escape from him." (1 Sam. 27:1)

In that moment, David did not tell himself the truth. Saul was not going to sweep him away. God had promised David would be king, and Saul could not thwart God's promise. In the meantime, David was counting days, wondering how long he could persevere, and crying out to God to act.

We stand with David and others determined to wait for God and for His perfect timing. We wonder when God will execute judgment but remain confident He will. We continue the countdown, watching with faith to see how God will fulfill His promises.

Day 4

Pits

The arrogant have dug pits for me; they violate Your instruction. All Your commands are true; people persecute me with lies—help me! (Ps. 119:85–86)

Some people view others with arrogance. They dig pits in the path, hoping the objects of their scorn will fall. Like dogs driving prey toward the net, the arrogant harass their targets with lies. They hope to upset those they despise, sending them running toward harm.

To drive others into pits, people must be calloused. Self-centered arrogance enables them to trivialize people and toy with them. Spiritual arrogance hardens them against God's instruction and keeps them moving further from God.

Are you being hounded toward a hidden pit? Take consolation. You're in noble company. King David often expressed his frustration about those who tried to entrap him.

They hid their net for me without cause; they dug a pit for me without cause. (Ps. 35:7)

Those who seek my life set traps, and those who want to harm me threaten to destroy me; they plot treachery all day long. (Ps. 38:12)

Even Jesus spent years in ministry tangling with religious leaders trying to trip Him up.

Then the Pharisees went and plotted how to trap Him by what He said. (Matt. 22:15)

Imagine the folly of trying to trap the Son of God. The Pharisees were arrogant enough to attempt it repeatedly. But why did they do that to Jesus? He knew the truth we must affirm. He confronted the Pharisees this way:

"You are of your father the Devil, and you want to carry out your father's desires. He was a murderer from the beginning and has not stood in the truth, because there is no truth in him. When he tells a lie, he speaks from his own nature, because he is a liar and the father of liars." (John 8:44)

Our spiritual enemy, Satan, will one day be thrown into the ultimate pit. Until then, if we are focused on God's commands, we can expect some pits in our path. Count this an honor.

Day 5

Almost

They almost ended my life on earth, but I did not abandon Your precepts. Give me life in accordance with Your faithful love, and I will obey the decree You have spoken. (Ps. 119:87–88)

In life, "almost" makes a big difference. If something is "almost," it's slightly short of, not quite, or nearly. You never want to be "almost killed," but "almost" beats the alternative.

The psalmist experienced that reality. So crushing were the pressures that he felt life slipping away. The gap between life and death remained only a crack.

Looking through that tiny gap, the psalmist affirmed God's precepts. In spite of the pressure, he remained true to God's Word. In desperation, he asked for a life aligned with God's faithful love. Whatever God's love dictated, that's what the psalmist wanted. The reason prompted the asking. He wanted more life so that he could obey God's decrees, all that God had revealed in His Word.

King David understood such pressure and prayed for insight into the duration of life.

"LORD, reveal to me the end of my life and the number of my days. Let me know how short-lived I am." (Ps. 39:4)

No matter how long we live, life on earth is short in the context of eternity. Our goal is to live God-focused lives of obedience motivated by love. We stand with the apostle Paul.

My eager expectation and hope is that I will not be ashamed about anything, but that now as always, with all boldness, Christ will be highly honored in my body, whether by life or by death. (Phil. 1:20)

For us, living is always "now" and "not yet." We seize every moment God gives us to honor Him. We endure now because God's Kingdom is coming; it's just not here yet. We're on our way home. No matter how long Jesus tarries, it's almost time. We'll see Him soon.

How Many Days
Psalm 119:81–88

Verse 1

I long for Your salvation, put my hope in Your word.
My eyes grow weary looking for what You've promised.
I ask, "When will You comfort me?"
Though I've become like a wineskin dried by smoke,
I do not forget, do not forget Your statutes.

Chorus

How many days must Your servant wait?

When will You execute judgment on my persecutors?

How many days must Your servant wait?

When will You execute judgment on my persecutors?

How many days? How many days? How many days must Your servant wait?

Verse 2

The arrogant have dug pits for me.

They violate, violate Your instruction.

All your commands are true.

People persecute me, persecute me with lies.

Help me! They almost ended my life.

Repeat Chorus

Bridge

Help me! Help me!

They almost ended my life on earth

But I did not abandon Your precepts.

Give me life in accordance with Your faithful love

And I will obey the decree You've spoken.

Final Chorus and Close

How many days must Your servant wait?

When will You execute judgment on my persecutors?

How many days must Your servant wait?

When will You execute judgment on my persecutors?

How many days? How many days? How many days must Your servant wait?

Chapter 12

Lord, Your Word Is Forever

LORD, *Your word is forever; it is firmly fixed in heaven.*

Your faithfulness is for all generations; You established the earth, and it stands firm.

They stand today in accordance with Your judgments, for all things are Your servants.

If Your instruction had not been my delight, I would have died in my affliction.

I will never forget Your precepts, for You have given me life through them.

I am Yours; save me, for I have sought Your precepts.

The wicked hope to destroy me, but I contemplate Your decrees.

I have seen a limit to all perfection, but Your command is without limit.

—Psalm 119:89–96

Day 1

Fixed

LORD, *Your word is forever; it is firmly fixed in heaven. Your faithfulness is for all generations; You established the earth, and it stands firm. (Ps. 119:89–90)*

When ships navigate ocean waters they use a fixed point such as a star to determine their current position. With no fixed point for reference, sailors become disoriented. We face the same challenges in our lives.

God is our fixed point. He stands above all we experience so we can look to Him and gain our bearings.

The LORD reigns! He is robed in majesty; The LORD is robed, enveloped in strength. The world is firmly established; it cannot be shaken. Your throne has been established from the beginning; You are from eternity. (Ps. 93:1–2)

Our focus on God is not subjective. His Word, the Bible, is fixed in heaven, telling us of His faithfulness and confirming His consistent actions for centuries of human history.

In addition to God's Word, creation points us to the Creator. God has given some people great intellectual capabilities. Theoretical physicists, for example, develop intricate theories about the origins of the cosmos. At times, some attempt to cross the line beyond which only God can stand. Job once crossed that line, and God confronted him.

Who is this who obscures My counsel with ignorant words? Get ready to answer Me like a man; when I question you, you will inform Me. Where were you when I established the earth? Tell Me, if you have understanding. Who fixed its dimensions? Certainly you know! Who stretched a measuring line across it? What supports its foundations? Or who laid its cornerstone while the morning stars sang together and all the sons of God shouted for joy? (Job 38:2–7)

We live in a world of mystery explained by the providence of God and held by His absolute power. As we move through time and eternity, He alone is our fixed point.

Day 2

Accordance

They stand today in accordance with Your judgments, for all things are Your servants. If Your instruction had not been my delight, I would have died in my affliction. (Ps. 119:91–92)

We marvel at the internal consistency of God's Word. The specific judgments we find in one part of the Bible find completion in the totality of God's revelation. All of God's Word serves all of God's purposes.

During the years the Israelites lived as exiles in Babylon, the prophet Daniel struggled to understand God's plan. Fortunately, he had a copy of the inspired words spoken by the prophet Jeremiah. As he studied, Daniel gained insight.

In the first year of his reign, I, Daniel, understood from the books according to the word of the LORD to Jeremiah the prophet that the number of years for the desolation of Jerusalem would be 70. So I turned my attention to the Lord God to seek Him by prayer and petitions, with fasting, sackcloth, and ashes. (Dan. 9:2–3)

Since he knew the duration of the exile, Daniel turned to God, seeking to make any adjustments necessary to align with God's plans. We now have a complete Bible. Our opportunities to live in accordance with God's Word are even more significant.

> *Now to Him who has power to strengthen you according to my gospel and the proclamation about Jesus Christ, according to the revelation of the mystery kept silent for long ages but now revealed and made known through the prophetic Scriptures, according to the command of the eternal God to advance the obedience of faith among all nations—to the only wise God, through Jesus Christ—to Him be the glory forever! Amen. (Rom. 16:25–27)*

Without God's Word, affliction would leave us hopeless. By faith, now we trust that God is aligning all things in accordance with His ultimate plans and good purposes.

Day 3

Given

> *I will never forget Your precepts, for You have given me life through them. (Ps. 119:93)*

God has given us His Word, His precepts to follow. We value the physical expressions of these words, the Bibles that hold them or the art that presents them. We recognize, though, that the power is not in print on paper. God's power flows to those who go where the words point and do what the words command.

Ultimately, all of God's Word points to Jesus. Even in the Old Testament, the prophet Isaiah spoke of the One to come, given for the world.

> *For a child will be born for us, a son will be given to us, and the government will be on His shoulders. He will be named*

Wonderful Counselor, Mighty God, Eternal Father, Prince of Peace. (Isa. 9:6)

Years later, the apostle Paul would speak of Jesus, the One who came to fulfill the Law and all that was promised in the Old Testament. This One gave us life.

I have been crucified with Christ and I no longer live, but Christ lives in me. The life I now live in the body, I live by faith in the Son of God, who loved me and gave Himself for me. (Gal. 2:19–20)

It is inconceivable for us to forget God's Word because the Word speaks of Christ, the key to our lives.

And we know that the Son of God has come and has given us understanding so that we may know the true One. We are in the true One—that is, in His Son Jesus Christ. He is the true God and eternal life. (1 John 5:20)

We live a "given" life. In God's great mercy, He promised. In God's great faithfulness, He fulfilled His promise through Jesus. We live now because God has given us life.

Day 4

Contemplate

I am Yours; save me, for I have sought Your precepts. The wicked hope to destroy me, but I contemplate Your decrees. (Ps. 119:94–95)

Even if we read the entire Bible one thousand times, we could never grasp the full magnitude of God's gracious revelation to us. So substantive is God's truth that we must savor it, reflect on it, and let its implications course through our hearts. The Bible affirms the decision to contemplate God's Word.

How happy is the man who does not follow the advice of the wicked or take the path of sinners or join a group of mockers! Instead, his delight is in the LORD's instruction, and he meditates on it day and night. He is like a tree planted beside streams of water that bears its fruit in season and whose leaf does not wither. Whatever he does prospers. (Ps. 1:1–3)

How different is the way of the wicked, those who despise others who set their hope on God.

The wicked are not like this; instead, they are like chaff that the wind blows away. Therefore the wicked will not survive the judgment, and sinners will not be in the community of the righteous. (Ps. 1:4–5)

We cannot control how other people respond to us. Evil people may actually hope to destroy us. What are we to do? If we allow them to dominate our lives, we empower them. Our fear strengthens them. By changing our focus, we diminish them by meditating on God's decrees. In the Bible, we discover God's ultimate plans for the wicked, His commitment to stand for the weak, and His promised justice for evil.

God, within Your temple, we contemplate Your faithful love. (Ps. 48:9)

This is worship—contemplating the magnificent truth that God has revealed to us.

Day 5

Perfection

I have seen a limit to all perfection, but Your command is without limit. (Ps. 119:96)

In this world we speak of perfection—a perfect diamond, a perfect day, a perfect ending. We actually mean superior to others, better than expected. We do not mean completely without flaw.

The lack of the "perfect" does not stop us from looking. Our idea of "perfection" is a gift from God, faint and fleeting, something that whispers to us about His absolute purity. This is the testimony throughout the Bible.

For I will proclaim Yahweh's name. Declare the greatness of our God! The Rock—His work is perfect; all His ways are entirely just. A faithful God, without prejudice, He is righteous and true. (Deut. 32:3–4)

God—His way is perfect; the word of the LORD is pure. He is a shield to all who take refuge in Him. For who is God besides the LORD? And who is a rock? Only our God. God is my strong refuge; He makes my way perfect. He makes my feet like the feet of a deer and sets me securely on the heights. (2 Sam. 22:31–34)

The instruction of the LORD is perfect, renewing one's life; the testimony of the LORD is trustworthy, making the inexperienced wise. (Ps. 19:7)

God's perfection is a big problem for us. People hear about sin and assume that God will judge on a sliding scale with everyone ranked "above average." That assumption is fatally flawed. Jesus explained God's standard:

Be perfect, therefore, as your heavenly Father is perfect. (Matt. 5:48)

The requirements of God's commands are without limit. As a result, none of us could measure up. In a jumping contest over the Grand Canyon, some may jump further, but all fall short. So it is with God's standard. Jesus came as our substitute perfection. He met God's ultimate standard. Because He was perfect, we can be counted perfect before God in Jesus.

Lord, Your Word Is Forever
Psalm 119:89–96

Chorus

LORD, Your word is forever. It's firmly fixed in heaven.

Your faithfulness is for all generations. You established the earth, and it stands firm.

LORD, Your word is forever.

Verse 1

They stand today in accordance with Your judgments,

For all things are Your servants.

If Your instruction had not been my delight,

I would have died in my affliction.

Repeat Chorus

Verse 2

I will never forget Your precepts.

You've given me life through them.

I am Yours; save me,

for I have sought Your precepts.

Bridge

The wicked hope to destroy me, but I contemplate Your decrees.

I've seen a limit to all perfection, but Your command is without limit.

Final Verse and Close

LORD, Your word is forever. It's firmly fixed in heaven.

Your faithfulness is for all generations. You established the earth, and it stands firm.

LORD, Your word is forever. LORD, Your word is forever.

Chapter 13

How Sweet Your Word

How I love Your teaching! It is my meditation all day long.

Your command makes me wiser than my enemies, for it is always with me.

I have more insight than all my teachers because Your decrees are my meditation.

I understand more than the elders because I obey Your precepts.

I have kept my feet from every evil path to follow Your word.

I have not turned from Your judgments, for You Yourself have instructed me.

How sweet Your word is to my taste—sweeter than honey to my mouth.

I gain understanding from Your precepts; therefore I hate every false way.

—Psalm 119:97–104

Day 1

Comparisons

How I love Your teaching! It is my meditation all day long. Your command makes me wiser than my enemies, for it is always with me. (Ps. 119:97–98)

From an early age we begin comparing ourselves. Children want to determine who is the tallest or fastest. Later we compare abilities—the smartest, the best at sports, the "first chair" musician. Over time, people calculate who is the most successful, has the most money, the most friends, the best life. The apostle Paul warned against comparisons:

For we don't dare classify or compare ourselves with some who commend themselves. But in measuring themselves by themselves and comparing themselves to themselves, they lack understanding. (2 Cor. 10:12)

While God's Word warns us against arbitrary comparisons, it affirms the desire to increase in wisdom. The psalmist noted that God increases the wisdom of His followers so they can prevail against their enemies. Increased wisdom requires excellent instruction.

Instruct a wise man, and he will be wiser still; teach a righteous man, and he will learn more. (Prov. 9:9)

Through the Bible, God teaches us. He provides ongoing instruction 24/7/365 to all who want to learn. When not "in class" by reading and studying God's Word, we have the opportunity to meditate on the truth, reflect on it, and mull it over until its implications penetrate our minds and hearts.

Only God's commands give us true spiritual wisdom. They are always available to us in the Bible and always with us as we learn the truth and base our lives on it. The depth of our wisdom corresponds to the breadth of our knowledge of God's Word. The equation is simple but profound: more of God's Word equals more wisdom. It's good to be wiser than our enemies. It's far better to be wiser than we were before— a day ago, a week ago, or a year ago—because God is teaching us through His Word. That comparison matters.

Day 2

Insight

I have more insight than all my teachers because Your decrees are my meditation. I understand more than the elders because I obey Your precepts. (Ps. 119:99–100)

It's difficult to draw a hard-edged technical distinction between "insight" and "understanding." Here's one way to think about the difference. Someone can understand without gaining insight, but insight requires understanding. People with insight draw on all they have studied, learned, experienced, and understood to then discern the true nature of a situation, perhaps one they have not encountered before.

Once in Babylon in the midst of a debauched banquet, the hand of God wrote on the wall as the king and his guests watched. The tone of the party changed. The king searched for anyone who could tell him the meaning. Ultimately, he called for Daniel, one of the Jewish exiles, an old man at this point who had spent his life seeking God and worshipping Him.

Then Daniel was brought before the king. The king said to him, "Are you Daniel, one of the Judean exiles that my predecessor the king brought from Judah? I've heard that you have the spirit of the gods in you, and that you have insight, intelligence, and extraordinary wisdom." (Dan. 5:13–14)

As He had done many times before, God gave Daniel insight and enabled him to explain the meaning of the writing. Daniel was a unique man of God. That moment was extraordinary. We cannot presume that God will work through us in the same way He did through Daniel. However, we must not put Daniel in an elite group to be admired but not emulated.

Comparing ourselves with our teachers is not prideful if we use them as a ruler. We don't brag when we grow; we simply note the change. Spiritual growth comes from studying and learning, meditating and reflecting, understanding and obeying God's Word. Daniel exemplified this spiritual posture. We must make God and His Word the priority in our lives as Daniel did. Then God can bless us with insight into the times in which we live.

Day 3

Decisions

I have kept my feet from every evil path to follow Your word. I have not turned from Your judgments, for You Yourself have instructed me. (Ps. 119:101–102)

The lives we live flow from the decisions we make. The prophet Isaiah described people who stubbornly moved down the wrong path.

Their feet run after evil, and they rush to shed innocent blood. Their thoughts are sinful thoughts; ruin and wretchedness are in their paths. They have not known the path of peace, and there is no justice in their ways. They have made their roads crooked; no one who walks on them will know peace. (Isa. 59:7–8)

Sometimes the destination of a particular path is not evident. Many times, though, the end is clear from the beginning. Solomon warned of the folly of traveling clearly evil paths.

Don't set foot on the path of the wicked; don't proceed in the way of evil ones. (Prov. 4:14)

One of the primary functions of God's Word is to help us see where life's paths lead. God instructs us about where to go and what to avoid. He identifies good traveling companions and those who bring only trouble.

People muse about how their lives will turn out. Clearly, we cannot predict that, but our decisions rule out many potential problems. If you decide not to fly in a tiny plane, you can be sure you will not die in a tiny plane. If you remain faithful to your spouse, you will avoid the pain that comes with adultery. If you do not steal, you will not be punished as a thief. If you decide to tell the truth, you don't have to worry about keeping your story straight.

God's Word tells us the benefits of going God's way. God's Spirit empowers us to make the right decisions, avoiding evil paths and doing as He has instructed. The story of our lives will be defined by the decisions we make about the paths we will travel.

Day 4

Acquired

How sweet Your word is to my taste—sweeter than honey to my mouth. (Ps. 119:103)

Sometimes we acquire a taste for certain drinks or foods that we did not have initially. The first time some people taste coffee, they find it disgusting. Over time, some of these same people learn to love coffee. They change, enjoying the taste of something that had repulsed them initially. Of course, the process can work the other way round.

During the years the Israelites wandered in the wilderness, God fed them with manna.

The manna resembled coriander seed, and its appearance was like that of bdellium. The people walked around and gathered it. They ground it on a pair of grinding stones or crushed it in a mortar, then boiled it in a cooking pot and shaped it into cakes. It tasted like a pastry cooked with the finest oil. (Num. 11:7–8)

What the people enjoyed initially lost its attraction over the years.

Contemptible people among them had a strong craving for other food. The Israelites cried again and said, "Who will feed us meat? We remember the free fish we ate in Egypt, along with the cucumbers, melons, leeks, onions, and garlic. But now our appetite is gone; there's nothing to look at but this manna!" (Num. 11:4–6)

God feeds His people through His Word. If our spiritual taste buds are working, we should find God's Word sweet, almost like honey. But what if that's not our first impression? No problem; we simply continue to read the Bible until we acquire a taste for it.

The greater danger, though, may be shifting into reverse, like the people in the wilderness. Those who have enjoyed a steady diet of God's Word for years can grow tired of it. Hopefully, such experiences are limited and fleeting. Even if we continue to struggle, we must take in God's Word regularly. Without food and water, we die physically. Without God's Word we wither spiritually. Ask God to make His Word sweet to you.

Day 5

Therefore

I gain understanding from Your precepts; therefore I hate every false way. (Ps. 119:104)

Never skip over the word "therefore." It connects what comes before with what comes after. Because the psalmist understood God's precepts, he hated every false way.

It's the same for us. God's precepts give us understanding. Things that once perplexed us become clear. We can see how puzzling events fit together and what "causes" yield specific "effects." Rather than bumping along blindly in life, we can live proactively.

Our understanding makes "therefores" possible.

We can therefore distinguish between a *false way* and a *true way*. Don't underestimate the value here. If people cannot recognize the marks of a false way, they can spend years moving blindly down the wrong road, missing the warning signals and flashing lights. Not so for those with understanding. They can spot a false way because it stands in clear contrast with the true way revealed in God's Word.

We can therefore identify *every* false way. What makes a way false? It varies. Evil morphs. It may take different forms over the years. With God's precepts to guide us, we can diagnose what we are facing and avoid what is false. Armed with God's Word, we can prepare for *every* false way we will encounter no matter what disguise evil wears.

We can therefore *hate* every false way. Those who have gained understanding from God's Word do not simply avoid evil ways; they hate them. They recognize the damage evil inflicts on people. They know the destruction and pain. Even more, they live with the knowledge that there is an alternative. In the end, there are two ways.

"For everyone who practices wicked things hates the light and avoids it, so that his deeds may not be exposed. But anyone who lives by the truth comes to the light, so that his works may be shown to be accomplished by God." (John 3:20–21)

Therefore, let us hate the darkness and love the light revealed in God's Word.

How Sweet Your Word
Psalm 119:97–104

Verse 1

How I love Your teaching! It's my meditation.

My meditation all day long.

Your command makes me wiser, wiser than my enemies

for it's always with me; it's with me.

Chorus

How sweet Your word.

Sweeter than honey to my taste; sweeter than honey to my mouth.

I gain understanding from Your precepts; therefore I hate every false way.

How sweet Your word; sweeter than honey to my mouth.

Verse 2

I have more insight than all my teachers

'cause Your decrees are my meditation.

I understand more than the elders

'cause I obey Your precepts.

Repeat Chorus

Bridge

I have kept my feet from every evil path to follow Your word, follow Your word.

I have not turned from Your judgments for You; You, Yourself have instructed me.

Repeat Verse 1

Repeat Chorus and Close

How sweet Your word.

Sweeter than honey to my taste; sweeter than honey to my mouth.

I gain understanding from Your precepts; therefore I hate every false way.

How sweet Your word;

sweeter than honey, sweeter than honey to my mouth.

Chapter 14

Your Decrees as a Heritage

Your word is a lamp for my feet and a light on my path.

I have solemnly sworn to keep Your righteous judgments.

I am severely afflicted; LORD, give me life through Your word.

LORD, please accept my willing offerings of praise, and teach me Your judgments.

My life is constantly in danger, yet I do not forget Your instruction.

The wicked have set a trap for me, but I have not wandered from Your precepts.

I have Your decrees as a heritage forever; indeed, they are the joy of my heart.

I am resolved to obey Your statutes to the very end.

—Psalm 119:105–112

Day 1

Lamp

Your word is a lamp for my feet and a light on my path.
(Ps. 119:105)

Darkness frightens and complicates. It is one of life's default modes. Remove light and you get darkness; add light and darkness ends. We associate lamps with light; but a lamp is a means to light, not light itself. Enter a dark room with an unlit lamp and you'll stand in the dark.

God's Word is a lamp that guides us as we walk and move down a path. But what is the connection between God's Word as a lamp and the light it produces? At the risk of over-simplification, it's helpful to think of God's Word as our lamp and God as our light.

The prophet Isaiah foretold a great light to come according to God's promise:

The people walking in darkness have seen a great light; a light has dawned on those living in the land of darkness. (Isa. 9:2)

Consistent with this prophecy, the apostle John described Jesus' ministry this way.

Life was in Him, and that life was the light of men. That light shines in the darkness, yet the darkness did not overcome it. (John 1:4–5)

As Jesus explained His ministry, He used the analogy of light:

Then Jesus spoke to them again: "I am the light of the world. Anyone who follows Me will never walk in the darkness but will have the light of life." (John 8:12)

Speaking to His disciples, Jesus made a stunning statement:

"You are the light of the world. A city situated on a hill cannot be hidden." (Matt. 5:14)

What? Lamps, maybe. But lights? Yes, because Jesus opened the way to God that would make it possible for the Holy Spirit to live in His disciples. In this way, we become lit lamps shining the light of God. Could we have figured this out on our own? Could we have illuminated our own path through human wisdom? No, we needed the lamp of God's Word to tell us how the God of light could take up residence in our lives and shine through us.

Day 2

Solemnly

I have solemnly sworn to keep Your righteous judgments. I am severely afflicted; LORD, give me life through Your word. (Ps. 119:106–107)

In the Old Testament, oaths were common. For example, God made oaths to people.

But because the LORD loved you and kept the oath He swore to your fathers, He brought you out with a strong hand. (Deut. 7:8)

In the same way, people expressed their intention to obey God or to keep their word to others by taking an oath.

You are to fear Yahweh your God and worship Him. Remain faithful to Him and take oaths in His name. He is your praise and He is your God, who has done for you these great and awesome works your eyes have seen. (Deut. 10:20–21)

The psalmist stated his earnest, sober-minded intention to keep God's righteous judgments. To signify the seriousness of this commitment, he took an oath. Even in the face of affliction, he intended to obey God's Word. He knew that God's Word was life.

By the time of Jesus' ministry, oath-taking had become perfunctory, a complicated system of swearing by different things to give the oath-takers latitude to break their word. Jesus would have none of it and told His disciples to speak their intentions without oaths and then do what they said. The apostle James summarized this principle:

> Now above all, my brothers, do not swear, either by heaven or by earth or with any other oath. Your "yes" must be "yes," and your "no" must be "no," so that you won't fall under judgment. (James 5:12)

We understand the significance of God's Word and want to obey it. Perfect obedience is not possible, so oaths are not appropriate. We simply state our intention. If we fail, God forgives. God is pleased with our desire to obey and our solemn commitment to do so . . . no matter how imperfectly.

Day 3

Willing

LORD, please accept my willing offerings of praise, and teach me Your judgments. (Ps. 119:108)

Imagine a rich person who lacks nothing. Now picture a young relative bringing a gift, a trinket in comparative terms, but handing it over mumbling, "I don't see why I have to give this." The entire experience is a washout. The rich relative didn't need the gift; delight would come only by the manner in which it was given.

With God, the disparity between the recipient and the giver is infinitely greater. We can give God nothing that He needs, only what He deserves.

Each person should do as he has decided in his heart—not reluctantly or out of necessity, for God loves a cheerful giver. (2 Cor. 9:7)

In reality, the best gift we give God is the manner in which we give. If we do not give willingly and joyfully, there is no reason God should accept. The loss is ours, not God's. The writer of Hebrews affirms the value of giving God the gift of praise:

Therefore, through Him let us continually offer up to God a sacrifice of praise, that is, the fruit of our lips that confess His name. (Heb. 13:15)

God understands our limitations. He knows that sometimes we struggle to give joyfully, so He accepts our sacrifice of praise as an act of obedience. Our giving professes, "Jesus is Lord." Over time, professing, confessing, and giving prompt praise.

As we give to God, He teaches us more about His Word. God's commands convince us that earning favor with God is impossible. Our only hope is God giving us a gift.

For the wages of sin is death, but the gift of God is eternal life in Christ Jesus our Lord. (Rom. 6:23)

God freely gave His only Son. Understanding the tiniest bit of that incredible reality prompts us to praise—willingly, joyfully, and continually.

Day 4

Danger

My life is constantly in danger, yet I do not forget Your instruction. The wicked have set a trap for me, but I have not wandered from Your precepts. (Ps. 119:109–110)

Our world is dangerous. The possibility of suffering harm or injury is real. To survive, many stuff thoughts of danger into compartments of the heart and attempt to manage their outbreaks. There is a better way. The apostle Paul lived the alternative. Looking back over his life of ministry, here's how he described it:

Five times I received 39 lashes from Jews. Three times I was beaten with rods by the Romans. Once I was stoned by my enemies. Three times I was shipwrecked. I have spent a night and a day in the open sea. On frequent journeys, I faced dangers from rivers, dangers from robbers, dangers from my own people, dangers from the Gentiles, dangers in the city, dangers in the open country, dangers on the sea, and dangers among false brothers; labor and hardship, many sleepless nights, hunger and thirst, often without food, cold, and lacking clothing. (2 Cor. 11:24–27)

Danger did not deter Paul from the life to which God had called him. He did not seek a safe life, so he avoided controlled boredom. Like the psalmist, he acknowledged the danger he faced and lived constantly with an eye to God's instruction. The wicked were setting traps for him, but he did not run from them or wander from God's percepts. Paul was an extraordinary man, but God worked through him as God is willing to work through us.

Because the danger was real, Paul experienced fear. Once when he was in Corinth, God appeared to Paul in a vision to encourage him.

Then the Lord said to Paul in a night vision, "Don't be afraid, but keep on speaking and don't be silent. For I am with you, and no one will lay a hand on you to hurt you, because I have many people in this city." (Acts 18:9–10)

Fear is always the opposite of faith. We do not manage danger; we rely on God.

Day 5

Heritage

I have Your decrees as a heritage forever; indeed, they are the joy of my heart. I am resolved to obey Your statutes to the very end. (Ps. 119:111–112)

Many families enjoy a godly heritage. Older generations pass along items of value, stories, traditions, and standards for living. The ways of life from the earlier generation shape the lives of those who come after. Unfortunately, families can pass down an evil heritage as well as a good one. We find examples of both in the kings of Israel.

Jehoram was 32 years old when he became king and reigned eight years in Jerusalem. He walked in the way of the kings of Israel, as the house of Ahab had done, for Ahab's daughter was his wife. He did what was evil in the LORD's sight. (2 Chron. 21:5–6)

Josiah was eight years old when he became king and reigned 31 years in Jerusalem. He did what was right in the LORD's sight and walked in the ways of his ancestor David; he did not turn aside to the right or the left. (2 Chron. 34:1–2)

The writer of 2 Kings reflected on the life of Josiah and noted what made his life distinctive.

In addition, Josiah removed the mediums, the spiritists, household idols, images, and all the detestable things that were seen in the land of Judah and in Jerusalem. He did this in order to carry out the words of the law that were written in the book that Hilkiah the priest found in the LORD's temple. Before him there was no king like him who turned to the LORD with all his mind and with all his heart and with all his strength according to all the law of Moses, and no one like him arose after him. (2 Kings 23:24–25)

Our family heritage influences us but does not control us. By God's grace, we have God's decrees and we know God's truth. If God's Word becomes the joy of our lives and we resolve to obey His Word to the end of our days, we can reset our family heritage. As God works through us, we can pass along the invaluable gift of a godly heritage to the generations that come after us.

Your Decrees as a Heritage
Psalm 119:105–112

Verse 1

Your word is a lamp for my feet and a light on my path.
I have solemnly sworn to keep Your righteous judgments.
I am severely afflicted; LORD, give me life through Your word.

Chorus

I have Your decrees as a heritage, a heritage forever.

Indeed, they are the joy of my heart.

I am resolved to obey Your statutes to the very end.

I have Your decrees as a heritage, a heritage forever.

Verse 2

LORD, please accept my willing offerings of praise,

and teach me, teach me Your judgments.

My life's in constant danger, yet I don't forget Your instruction.

Repeat Chorus

Bridge

The wicked have set a trap for me,

but I have not wandered from, wandered from Your precepts.

Final Chorus and Close

I have Your decrees as a heritage, a heritage forever.

Indeed, they are the joy of my heart.

I am resolved to obey Your statutes to the very end.

I have Your decrees as a heritage, a heritage forever, a heritage forever.

Chapter 15

Sustain Me

I hate the double-minded, but I love Your instruction.

You are my shelter and my shield; I put my hope in Your word.

Depart from me, you evil ones, so that I may obey my God's commands.

Sustain me as You promised, and I will live; do not let me be ashamed of my hope.

Sustain me so that I can be safe and be concerned with Your statutes continually.

You reject all who stray from Your statutes, for their deceit is a lie.

You remove all the wicked on earth as if they were dross; therefore, I love Your decrees.

I tremble in awe of You; I fear Your judgments.

—Psalm 119:113–120

Day 1

Double-Minded

I hate the double-minded, but I love Your instruction. (Ps. 119:113)

Most of us can spot double-minded people. They waver and vacillate, exhibiting doubt and uncertainty. Decisions elude them because they draw from two minds at the same time. Get behind a double-minded person in the fast-food line and you're in for a wait. Getting stuck in line is one thing; getting stuck in life is another. The psalmist expressed his sentiment: "I hate the double-minded." It sounds like double-mindedness is more than an inconvenience.

Jesus gave one example of double-mindedness to help us recognize this malady:

"No one can be a slave of two masters, since either he will hate one and love the other, or be devoted to one and despise the other. You cannot be slaves of God and of money." (Matt. 6:24)

We cannot devote ourselves dually—to two things, people, ideals, values, whatever. People who desire to go in opposite directions at the same time get locked in place and go nowhere. Until they become single-minded, they remain unstable.

Why worry about the symptoms of double-mindedness without treating the underlying disease, a spiritual problem? The cure for double-mindedness is deceptively simple: single-mindedness. The psalmist knew the cure came from a clear focus on God's instruction, because deeply loving God's Word drives us to God.

Draw near to God, and He will draw near to you. Cleanse your hands, sinners, and purify your hearts, double-minded people! (James 4:8)

Spotting double-minded people is easy compared to dealing with the double-mindedness in our own hearts. Don't waste time hating what you see in others. Let's ask God to reveal the reality of this destructive bent in our own minds and hearts. Declare war on our double-mindedness by asking God to give us a single-minded love for His Word and for Him.

Day 2

Shelter

You are my shelter and my shield; I put my hope in Your word. Depart from me, you evil ones, so that I may obey my God's commands. (Ps. 119:114–115)

In a world pitched about by contradictory ideas, we find stability in God's Word. Secure with God, we can withstand the onslaught of the evil ones who come against us. The more they throw at us, the more we focus on our single-minded goal of obeying God's commands. As we obey, we experience God as our shelter and our shield.

When bad weather erupts, we take shelter temporarily to escape what has overtaken us. When the threat becomes more intense, shelter isn't enough; we need a shield from danger.

King David referred often to God as his shelter and his shield.

I will live in Your tent forever and take refuge under the shelter of Your wings. (Ps. 61:4)

I love You, LORD, my strength. The LORD is my rock, my fortress, and my deliverer, my God, my mountain where I seek refuge, my shield and the horn of my salvation, my stronghold. (Ps. 18:1–2)

In reality, God does not give us shelters and shields; He gives us Himself. The closer we move to Him, the more we are sheltered and the more fully He shields us. That's why David extolled God as the end of his quest for relief in times of trouble.

He said: The LORD is my rock, my fortress, and my deliverer, my God, my mountain where I seek refuge. My shield, the horn of my salvation, my stronghold, my refuge, and my Savior, You save me from violence. I called to the LORD, who is worthy of praise, and I was saved from my enemies. (2 Sam. 22:2–4)

Our double-minded enemies do not fear us. They can, however, recognize those who have found the ultimate refuge. Then they may think twice before they pick a fight with God to get to us.

Day 3

Sustain

Sustain me as You promised, and I will live; do not let me be ashamed of my hope. Sustain me so that I can be safe and be concerned with Your statutes continually. (Ps. 119:116–117)

In a crisis, we can do without many things. Minimum requirements though do exist for physical life, a certain amount of water, food, and air for example. The same principle applies to our spiritual lives. We have basic needs that we rely on God to supply.

For us to be sustained, we need God's Word—not just His general promises but His specific promises for what we face.

> *I lie down and sleep; I wake again because the LORD sustains me. I am not afraid of the thousands of people who have taken their stand against me on every side. (Ps. 3:5–6)*

For us to be sustained, we need spiritual hope. We must express confidence in God to keep His promises, unapologetic that we are relying on Him without a backup plan. Often, God's sustaining power enables us to press on through protracted trouble without buckling.

> *Cast your burden on the LORD, and He will sustain you; He will never allow the righteous to be shaken. (Ps. 55:22)*

For us to be sustained, though, we have to embrace God's view of safety.

> *We have this hope—like a sure and firm anchor of the soul—that enters the inner sanctuary behind the curtain. Jesus has entered there on our behalf as a forerunner, because He has become a "high priest forever." (Heb. 6:19–20)*

Many who focus on God and His Word do not experience physical safety in life. At best, safety is temporary. For us to be truly safe, we must be spiritually safe. That's what Jesus accomplished for us. He was the Great High Priest who made the ultimate sacrifice for us to open the way to God. Jesus is our promise; He is our hope. Our focus on God's Word reminds us that God's plan to sustain us is clear and sure—Jesus.

Day 4

Dross

You reject all who stray from Your statutes, for their deceit is a lie. You remove all the wicked on earth as if they were dross; therefore, I love Your decrees. (Ps. 119:118–119)

We live in a mixed-up, hodgepodge world of good and bad, wheat and chaff, good crops and weeds, silver and dross. Everything intertwines, defying anyone to separate the valuable from the waste.

Jesus told a parable about a landowner who sowed good seed in his field but later discovered that an enemy had sowed weeds secretly. The workers questioned the landowner about what to do with the weeds that were growing:

"'So, do you want us to go and gather them up?' the slaves asked him. "'No,' he said. 'When you gather up the weeds, you might also uproot the wheat with them. Let both grow together until the harvest. At harvest time I'll tell the reapers: Gather the weeds first and tie them in bundles to burn them, but store the wheat in my barn.'" (Matt. 13:28–30)

God knows the wicked. The objective standard of His statutes exposes cover-ups cloaked in lies. The wicked include those who shake their fists at God as well as those who simply wander without intention. The Bible's pages contain many references to the wicked, often about people questioning why God delays judgment on evil people.

LORD God of Hosts, You are the God of Israel, rise up to punish all the nations; do not show grace to any wicked traitors. (Ps. 59:5)

We know that apart from Christ, God must reject us. Only Jesus changed our classification from wicked to righteous.

We live as dross transferred out of the refuse pile and transformed. That's why we take the gospel to the wicked while the time for reclassification remains open before Jesus returns. Because we love God's decrees we do what He has decreed and share His good news with everyone.

Day 5

Tremble

I tremble in awe of You; I fear Your judgments. (Ps. 119:120)

God graciously gave people the capacity to tremble, to shake involuntarily with fear, anxiety, or the awareness of weakness. Trembling indicates our bodies are kicking into a higher gear, preparing for action as required. Think of trembling as high-alert status.

Some people fail to tremble. They evaluate a situation and deem it as common so they sashay along, flaunting their lack of concern. Are they brave? Not if a grizzly bear charges toward them. In that case, they need less sashay and more awe. Upping the awe should increase trembling and get them moving. Awe before a charging bear pales compared to the awe we should have for God.

Let the whole earth tremble before the LORD; let all the inhabitants of the world stand in awe of Him. (Ps. 33:8)

Worship the LORD in the splendor of His holiness; tremble before Him, all the earth. (Ps. 96:9)

The prophet Daniel prayed earnestly, asking God to forgive him and his people.

I prayed to the LORD my God and confessed: Ah, Lord— the great and awe-inspiring God who keeps His gracious covenant with those who love Him and keep His commands—we have sinned, done wrong, acted wickedly, rebelled, and turned away from Your commands and ordinances. (Dan. 9:4–5)

Christians fixate on God's love as if that wonderful trait is the most significant attribute of God. It isn't. We must understand God's love in the context of God's holiness. Only then will we respond appropriately. Studying God's Word gives us an increasingly clear picture of God based on His revelation. The more we learn, the greater our awe. Increased awe compels us to bow before Him with profound respect as we marvel that this God would love us by sending Jesus.

Sustain Me
Psalm 119:113–120

Verse 1

I hate the double-minded, but I love Your instruction.

You're my shelter and my shield.

I put my hope, put my hope in Your word.

Depart from me, you evil ones, so that I may obey my God's commands.

Chorus

Sustain me as You promised, sustain me and I will live.

Don't let me be ashamed of my hope. Sustain me so that I can be safe.

And be concerned with Your statutes continually. Sustain me.

Verse 2

You reject all who stray from Your statutes,
for their deceit, their deceit is a lie.
You remove all the wicked on earth,
the wicked as if they were dross; therefore, I love Your decrees.

Repeat Chorus

Bridge

I tremble, tremble in awe of you.
I fear your judgments and I tremble, tremble in awe of you.

Repeat Chorus and Close

Sustain me as You promised, sustain me and I will live.
Don't let me be ashamed of my hope. Sustain me so that I can be safe.
And be concerned with Your statutes continually.
Sustain me. Sustain me. Sustain me.

Chapter 16

My Eyes Grow Weary

I have done what is just and right; do not leave me to my oppressors.

Guarantee Your servant's well-being; do not let the arrogant oppress me.

My eyes grow weary looking for Your salvation and for Your righteous promise.

Deal with Your servant based on Your faithful love; teach me Your statutes.

I am Your servant; give me understanding so that I may know Your decrees.

It is time for the LORD to act, for they have broken Your law.

Since I love Your commandments more than gold, even the purest gold,

I carefully follow all Your precepts and hate every false way.

—*Psalm 119:121–128*

Day 1

Bewildered

I have done what is just and right; do not leave me to my oppressors. Guarantee Your servant's well-being; do not let the arrogant oppress me. (Ps. 119:121–122)

Life can bewilder us, leaving us disoriented and perplexed. Our expectations meter goes haywire. Things we expected do not happen; things not expected occur. We struggle to understand why. However imperfectly, we have tried to do what is just and right based on God's Word. Yet our opponents strengthen as we falter. Frankly, sometimes it feels like our opponents are a pack of wild dogs and God has left us to be devoured. Hanging by a faith thread, we continue to turn to God, asking for a guarantee that He will protect us. As His servants, we remind Him that currently the scoreboard indicates that the arrogant are winning.

The psalmist loved God's Word, studied it, meditated on it, and sought to understand its depths of meaning. That commitment, though, did not exempt him from spiritual bewilderment. While he confessed that God's Word was sweet as honey to him, he struggled to line up his reading with his experiences. He would have identified readily with the dark season Job passed through, asking pointed questions along the way.

What is man, that You think so highly of him and pay so much attention to him? You inspect him every morning, and put him to the test every moment. Will You ever look away from me, or leave me alone long enough to swallow? If I have sinned, what have I done to You, Watcher of mankind? Why have You made me Your target, so that I have become a burden to You? (Job 7:17–20)

God never explained Job's backstory to him. We know it, but Job didn't. In His grace, God allowed Job to write a primer on pain. Like the psalmist and Job, we need to know that loving God's Word does not give us a free pass out of pain. Instead of asking, "Why?" we learn to ask, "To what end?"

Day 2

Nothing

My eyes grow weary looking for Your salvation and for Your righteous promise. (Ps. 119:123)

Spiritual eyestrain occurs in people who watch for God's activity through faith. They know He is the source of salvation—saving us in eternity because of Christ but also saving us now. From a theological perspective, we have been saved, we are being saved, and we will be saved. God's righteous promises give basis for this hope.

Sometimes, though, we look and see nothing. We strain, turning to God's Word to help us see more clearly, to see further. At times, nothing comes into focus.

How can this be? Why would God allow His children to endure difficult circumstances without evidence of His presence, control, and blessing?

Think of Job. God stood with him through all that happened, exercising ultimate control. Satan could only do what God permitted. In time, God did bless Job again on earth.

So the LORD blessed the last part of Job's life more than the first. He owned 14,000 sheep, 6,000 camels, 1,000 yoke of oxen, and 1,000 female donkeys. He also had seven sons and three daughters. He named his first daughter Jemimah, his second Keziah, and his third Keren–happuch. No

women as beautiful as Job's daughters could be found in all
the land, and their father granted them an inheritance with
their brothers. Job lived 140 years after this and saw his
children and their children to the fourth generation. Then
Job died, old and full of days. (Job 42:12–17)

In reality, God blessed generations of believers through
Job's experience. All that happened to him and the manner
in which Job responded encourages us when we are spiritually exhausted. Job's life protects us from the false spiritual
expectation that things will always go well if we love God.
In His grace, God prepares us to confess that He is saving us
even when our experience denies our confession. It's okay to
look and see nothing.

Day 3

Dealing

Deal with Your servant based on Your faithful love; teach
me Your statutes. (Ps. 119:124)

Part of Job's suffering resulted from crummy friends.
While he suffered, Job's counselors hammered him with
spiritual drivel that God denounced in the end. Yet Job was
too sick to escape their theological blather. As Job's suffering
ended, God spoke directly to the friends and set the record
straight.

"Now take seven bulls and seven rams, go to My servant
Job, and offer a burnt offering for yourselves. Then My ser-
vant Job will pray for you. I will surely accept his prayer
and not deal with you as your folly deserves. For you have
not spoken the truth about Me, as My servant Job has."
Then Eliphaz the Temanite, Bildad the Shuhite, and Zophar

the Naamathite went and did as the LORD *had told them, and the* LORD *accepted Job's prayer. (Job 42:8–9)*

Fortunately for them, Job did not hold a grudge. He prayed for his friends, and God did not deal with them as they deserved. Fortunately, God deals with us in love as well. He extends grace as explained in His Word. King David experienced this reality.

But You, Yahweh my Lord, deal kindly with me because of Your name; deliver me because of the goodness of Your faithful love. (Ps. 109:21)

Without God's Word, we could not make sense of many of our experiences. With God's Word, questions remain but we gain perspective. Suffering morphs into a means God uses for positive change. The writer of Hebrews explained it this way:

Endure suffering as discipline: God is dealing with you as sons. For what son is there that a father does not discipline? (Heb. 12:7)

God's Word does not resolve all our questions. We do, however, learn to look at life through the lens of God's faithful love, trusting Him for purposeful outcomes as He deals with us.

Day 4

Now

I am Your servant; give me understanding so that I may know Your decrees. It is time for the LORD *to act, for they have broken Your law. (Ps. 119:125–126)*

Waiting in hope and responding in faith sound great, but sometimes we simply want God to act. As His servants, we seek understanding so we can know His decrees and what He has committed to do. Armed with that insight, we take note of wicked people who have broken God's law. Our minds swirl with questions that leave us muttering, "It's time for the Lord to act." We know God can act. For the life of us, we cannot imagine why He doesn't do something. King David struggled with this perplexing question of timing.

> LORD, why do You stand so far away? Why do You hide in times of trouble? (Ps. 10:1)

Unfortunately, we consistently miscalculate "now" time. We want God to act immediately or at least sooner than He does. For example, after Jesus was raised from the dead, He met with His disciples. In the face of this miracle, they questioned Him about their top-of-mind "now" issue. Notice how Jesus responded:

> So when they had come together, they asked Him, "Lord, are You restoring the kingdom to Israel at this time?" He said to them, "It is not for you to know times or periods that the Father has set by His own authority. But you will receive power when the Holy Spirit has come on you, and you will be My witnesses in Jerusalem, in all Judea and Samaria, and to the ends of the earth." (Acts 1:6–8)

Most things in our spiritual lives take longer than we prefer and longer than we think is right. Seeing the wicked continue with impunity perplexes us. Over time, we learn to rely on what God has revealed in His word, trusting it is sufficient. Rather than peppering God with questions about His time line, we can wait for His power. His power gives us the capacity to wait for God's "now"—the perfect moment when He acts.

Day 5

Since

Since I love Your commandments more than gold, even the purest gold, I carefully follow all Your precepts and hate every false way. (Ps. 119:127–128)

Loving God's commandments does good things in our lives spiritually. We understand that God's truth is more valuable than material riches, not just metaphorically but actually. Given the choice between more truth or more money, we can recognize the best option. Because of God's Word, we know what God expects and can align our lives increasingly with His precepts. As we learn more, God's Word gives us the capacity to recognize the false from the true in ourselves and in others.

All the good things the psalmist mentioned sprang from his love for God's Word—that was the "since." It is the same for us. That's why we strive to understand God's Word and teach it correctly. We long to live as workers that God approves.

Be diligent to present yourself approved to God, a worker who doesn't need to be ashamed, correctly teaching the word of truth. (2 Tim. 2:15)

Handling God's Word appropriately challenges the most diligent disciple. We long for God's approval. We don't want to be ashamed of what we have said about God, especially in times of pain and suffering, our own or that of others.

A straightforward reading of the Bible gives us enough truth to navigate life. God did not give us precise answers to every question. If we had needed more revelation, God would have given us more.

Loving God's commandments motivates us to look deeply into God's Word. No matter how many times we have read a portion of Scripture, new experiences help us see truth we missed earlier. God's Word explains our experiences; our experiences do not explain God's Word. Our questions begin with this declaration, "Since I love your commandments . . ." That's why we know where to look for answers.

My Eyes Grow Weary
Psalm 119:121–128

Verse 1

I have done what is just, and I've done what's right;
don't leave me to my oppressors.
Guarantee Your servant's well-being;
don't let the arrogant oppress me.

Chorus

My eyes grow weary looking for Your salvation and Your righteous promise.
Deal with Your servant based on Your faithful love; teach me Your statutes.
My eyes grow weary looking.

Verse 2

I am Your servant; give me understanding
so that I may know Your decrees.
It is time for the LORD to act,
for they have broken Your law.

Repeat Chorus

Bridge

Since I love Your commandments more than gold,
even the purest gold,
I carefully follow all Your precepts and hate every false
way.

Close

But my eyes grow weary looking for Your salvation,
my eyes grow weary looking.

Chapter 17

I Pant for Your Word

Your decrees are wonderful; therefore I obey them.

The revelation of Your words brings light and gives understanding to the inexperienced.

I pant with open mouth because I long for Your commands.

Turn to me and be gracious to me, as is Your practice toward those who love Your name.

Make my steps steady through Your promise; don't let sin dominate me.

Redeem me from human oppression, and I will keep Your precepts.

Show favor to Your servant, and teach me Your statutes.

My eyes pour out streams of tears because people do not follow Your instruction.

—Psalm 119:129–136

Day 1

Inexperienced

Your decrees are wonderful; therefore I obey them. The revelation of Your words brings light and gives understanding to the inexperienced. (Ps. 119:129–130)

Experience teaches us but gives the lesson *after* the test. If we could only learn through firsthand experience, few of us would survive. The tuition for an experiential education is steep. Solomon gave us a clear case study of inexperience leading to a crash.

At the window of my house I looked through my lattice. I saw among the inexperienced, I noticed among the youths, a young man lacking sense. Crossing the street near her corner, he strolled down the road to her house at twilight, in the evening, in the dark of the night. A woman came to meet him dressed like a prostitute, having a hidden agenda. (Prov. 7:6–10)

God's Word guards us against the danger that comes with inexperience. When we recognize God's decrees as wonderful and obey them, God illuminates our minds with His truth. In the process, we gain understanding. Awareness is not enough; we must act on God's Word. Only then will we grow up as Christians.

The writer of Hebrews explains that spiritual growth is expected and normal. He compared God's Word to nourishment, contrasting milk with solid food as a means to growth.

Although by this time you ought to be teachers, you need someone to teach you the basic principles of God's revelation again. You need milk, not solid food. Now everyone who lives on milk is inexperienced with the message about righteousness, because he is an infant. But solid food is for the mature—for those whose senses have been trained to distinguish between good and evil. (Heb. 5:12–14)

What we need is experience without the experience. God's Word allows us to audit the tough experiences of others, to learn from their examples, and to follow God's Word with wisdom.

Day 2

Panting

I pant with open mouth because I long for Your commands. Turn to me and be gracious to me, as is Your practice toward those who love Your name. (Ps. 119:131–132)

Breathing sustains life. Block access to air and we die. In his time of misery, Job spoke of the brevity of life, comparing life to a single breath.

My days pass more swiftly than a weaver's shuttle; they come to an end without hope. Remember that my life is but a breath. My eye will never again see anything good. (Job 7:6–7)

If exertion diminishes our oxygen levels, we gasp for breath. Opening our mouths wide, we gulp cold, sweet air. The oxygen works quickly in our system to restore our bodies.

In the same way that we breathe to live; we live to honor God and praise Him.

Let everything that breathes praise the LORD. Hallelujah! (Ps. 150:6)

God's Word is essential for spiritual life.

The psalmist centered his life on this truth. He recognized the value of God's Word and longed for it, panting for more.

He asked God to turn to him and be gracious. He did not presume on God's favor, but focused on God's practice of responding to those who love His name.

When we cannot get enough air, we gasp, panting until our need subsides. No one congratulates us for panting well. The response is involuntary. Our bodies recognize the need and respond automatically. In contrast, panting for God's Word is voluntary. We recognize our need and draw in the rejuvenating oxygen of God's Word so our souls can thrive.

Because panting for God's Word is mandatory, it is not praiseworthy. We pant spiritually because we recognize that we must have steady and increasing levels of God's Word in our lives to survive. God graciously provides all we need. We must breathe it in.

Day 3

Steady

Make my steps steady through Your promise . . .
(Ps. 119:133)

We desire lives that are steady—firmly fixed, supported, secure, and balanced. Oftentimes, we experience the opposite. Our worlds wobble. We stumble, attempting to brace ourselves against a fall. Just about the time we regain our balance, everything tilts and we lurch in another direction. Fortunately, even when everything shakes, we know the God of the Bible who holds all things in place.

We give thanks to You, God; we give thanks to You, for Your name is near. People tell about Your wonderful works. "When I choose a time, I will judge fairly. When the earth and all its inhabitants shake, I am the One who steadies its pillars." (Ps. 75:1–3)

In spite of God's sustaining work in the cosmos, we feel tossed about, unable to stabilize our lives. This churning prompts us to pursue God more desperately. The prophet Isaiah encouraged the people in their distress with these words.

It [the wilderness] will blossom abundantly and will also rejoice with joy and singing. The glory of Lebanon will be given to it, the splendor of Carmel and Sharon. They will see the glory of the LORD, the splendor of our God. Strengthen the weak hands, steady the shaking knees! Say to the cowardly: "Be strong; do not fear! Here is your God; vengeance is coming. God's retribution is coming; He will save you." (Isa. 35:2–4)

Our focus on God and His promises sustains us. As things around us roll, we cling securely to what God has said He will do.

Cast your burden on the LORD, and He will sustain you; He will never allow the righteous to be shaken. (Ps. 55:22)

God does not promise us smooth lives in which we walk with ease. He allows us to walk through seismic shocks with steady hearts as a testimony to His fortifying power.

Day 4

Domination

Don't let sin dominate me. Redeem me from human oppression, and I will keep Your precepts. (Ps. 119:133–134)

The shockwave created by the first sin in Eden engulfed the brothers, Cain and Abel. After God accepted Abel's sacrifice, God warned Cain about the danger of sin.

*Then the LORD said to Cain, "Why are you furious? And
why do you look despondent? If you do what is right, won't
you be accepted? But if you do not do what is right, sin is
crouching at the door. Its desire is for you, but you must rule
over it." (Gen. 4:6–7)*

Instead of changing his offering, Cain murdered his
brother. Rather than ruling sin, Cain allowed sin to rule him
with awful force. Defeat led to slavery.

*Since people are enslaved to whatever defeats them. (2 Pet.
2:19)*

We cannot see "sin." We only see its effects. As leaves
move, we can tell the wind is blowing. As people oppress others, we can tell sin is doing its foul work.

The prophet Jeremiah experienced ruthless opposition as
the people of Israel resisted the Word of the Lord that he
spoke. Without God's fortification, Jeremiah would have
buckled.

*Then I will make you a fortified wall of bronze to this peo-
ple. They will fight against you but will not overcome you,
for I am with you to save you and deliver you. (Jer. 15:20)*

God rescued Jeremiah and returned him to the work to
which God had called him. Jeremiah's temporal salvation
foreshadowed the perfect redemption to come in Christ.

*Therefore, no condemnation now exists for those in Christ
Jesus, because the Spirit's law of life in Christ Jesus has set
you free from the law of sin and of death. (Rom. 8:1–2)*

Armed with God's Word, we can fight the force of sin in
our fallen world. We can do through Christ what Cain failed
to do—rule over sin. Sin cannot dominate us unless we fail
to use the power God has given us, the power we discover in
God's Word.

Day 5

Tears

Show favor to Your servant, and teach me Your statutes. My eyes pour out streams of tears because people do not follow Your instruction. (Ps. 119:135–136)

The Fall of the world through sin set people against God and against each other. Hurting people hurt other people. Oppressed by sin, people expressed depravity with cruel creativity. King David felt the sharp attack of relentless foes and called out to God.

I am weary from my groaning; with my tears I dampen my pillow and drench my bed every night. My eyes are swollen from grief; they grow old because of all my enemies. Depart from me, all evildoers, for the LORD has heard the sound of my weeping. The LORD has heard my plea for help; the LORD accepts my prayer. (Ps. 6:6–9)

In our trouble, we seek God's favor. In response, God favors us with His Word. The truth relieves us but explains that most people will not follow God's instructions most of the time. With so many people off course, lives crash with devastating results. Surrounded by pain, we can identify with the psalmist's prayer as he looked forward to a day of restoration after destruction.

Restore our fortunes, LORD, like watercourses in the Negev. Those who sow in tears will reap with shouts of joy. Though one goes along weeping, carrying the bag of seed, he will surely come back with shouts of joy, carrying his sheaves. (Ps. 126:4–6)

Sin entered our world and broke it. During His earthly ministry, Jesus endured the world's pain so He could fix what sin had shattered.

During His earthly life, He offered prayers and appeals with loud cries and tears to the One who was able to save Him from death, and He was heard because of His reverence. Though He was God's Son, He learned obedience through what He suffered. (Heb. 5:7–8)

God repaired our hearts through Christ, removing sin's leverage in death. We cry now for those not yet released from sin, and pray for God's favor toward them in His mercy.

I Pant for Your Word
Psalm 119:129–136

Verse 1

Your decrees are wonderful therefore I obey them.
The revelation of Your words brings light
and gives understanding to the inexperienced.

Chorus

I pant with open mouth; I long for Your commands.
Turn to me and be gracious to me
as is Your practice toward those who love, who love Your name.
I pant for Your word.

Verse 2

Make my steps steady through Your promise.
Don't let sin dominate me.
Redeem me from oppression, and I'll keep Your precepts.

Chorus

Bridge

Show favor to Your servant,

and teach me Your statutes.

My eyes pour out streams of tears

'cause people do not follow Your instruction.

Final Chorus and Close

I pant with open mouth; I long for Your commands.

Turn to me and be gracious to me

As is Your practice toward those who love, who love Your name.

I pant for Your word.

Chapter 18

Everlasting Righteousness

You are righteous, LORD, and Your judgments are just.

The decrees You issue are righteous and altogether trustworthy.

My anger overwhelms me because my foes forget Your words.

Your word is completely pure, and Your servant loves it.

I am insignificant and despised, but I do not forget Your precepts.

Your righteousness is an everlasting righteousness, and Your instruction is true.

Trouble and distress have overtaken me, but Your commands are my delight.

Your decrees are righteous forever. Give me understanding, and I will live.

—Psalm 119:137–144

Day 1

Righteous

You are righteous, LORD, and Your judgments are just. The decrees You issue are righteous and altogether trustworthy. (Ps. 119:137–138)

God is righteous—perfectly wonderful, fine, and genuine, free from any flaw. Until we recognize the righteousness of God we will struggle to acknowledge the truth of His Word or to understand our need to be declared righteous before Him.

As Moses explained God's law to the Israelites preparing to enter the Promised Land, he highlighted God's righteousness.

For I will proclaim Yahweh's name. Declare the greatness of our God! The Rock—His work is perfect; all His ways are entirely just. A faithful God, without prejudice, He is righteous and true. (Deut. 32:3–4)

The prophet Zechariah predicted the coming of Jesus and spoke of His righteousness.

Rejoice greatly, Daughter Zion! Shout in triumph, Daughter Jerusalem! Look, your King is coming to you; He is righteous and victorious, humble and riding on a donkey, on a colt, the foal of a donkey. (Zech. 9:9)

When Jesus prayed to His heavenly Father, He spoke of righteousness.

"Righteous Father! The world has not known You. However, I have known You, and these have known that You sent Me." (John 17:25)

The apostle John glimpsed the righteousness of Jesus in eternity.

They sang the song of God's servant Moses and the song of the Lamb: Great and awe-inspiring are Your works, Lord God, the Almighty; righteous and true are Your ways, King of the Nations. (Rev. 15:3)

Fathoming God's absolute righteousness exceeds our capacity. God's truth crushes our pretense and pride. His judgments and decrees confirm our hopeless unrighteousness and convict us to call for a Savior.

Day 2

Anger

My anger overwhelms me because my foes forget Your words. (Ps. 119:139)

Often we respond to others with annoyance, displeasure, hostility, or rage. Like a wildfire our anger blows and grows in intensity. Once unleashed, anger can consume, but its first fuel is the angry person. Controlling anger is a tricky business, but God shows us how.

The Bible explains that God grows angry at sin, even the sin of His children who respond to Him with stiff-necked rebellion. One psalmist worried that God would never stop being angry at Israel's disobedience.

Return to us, God of our salvation, and abandon Your displeasure with us. Will You be angry with us forever? Will You prolong Your anger for all generations? Will You not revive us again so that Your people may rejoice in You? (Ps. 85:4–6)

On the other hand, anger can be like fire in a pit, a purposeful blaze controlled for good.

Know that the LORD *has set apart the faithful for Himself;
the* LORD *will hear when I call to Him. Be angry and do
not sin; on your bed, reflect in your heart and be still.
(Ps. 4:3–4)*

Once Jesus confronted a group of Pharisees opposed to His
healing a man with a paralyzed hand on the Sabbath. Jesus
expressed anger without sin.

*Then He said to them, "Is it lawful on the Sabbath to do
what is good or to do what is evil, to save life or to kill?" But
they were silent. After looking around at them with anger
and sorrow at the hardness of their hearts, He told the man,
"Stretch out your hand." So he stretched it out, and his hand
was restored. (Mark 3:4–5)*

Sin should anger us, beginning with the sin we see in our
own hearts. If we grow angry at others, we must focus on
actions, not on people. We are not God, so we must express
anger with extreme care and never with self-righteous, self-
serving indignation. Only God sees clearly enough to judge
and is righteous enough to punish. Our anger requires a leash.

Day 3

Contrasts

*Your word is completely pure, and Your servant loves it. I
am insignificant and despised, but I do not forget Your precepts. (Ps. 119:140–141)*

Take a clear picture of the human race in our imperfections
and place it alongside God's Word. The contrast is striking.
God's Word is completely true, worthy of love and remem-
brance. In contrast, we are insignificant and often despised.

Any time we read God's Word, we learn more about God and get greater insight into ourselves. For example, when King David learned of the great promises God had made through the prophet, David prayed with amazement.

Because of Your word and according to Your will, You have revealed all these great things to Your servant. This is why You are great, Lord GOD. There is no one like You, and there is no God besides You, as all we have heard confirms. (2 Sam. 7:21–22)

All that God reveals about Himself should cause us to marvel at the infinite difference between Him and us.

The LORD reigns! Let the peoples tremble. He is enthroned above the cherubim. Let the earth quake. Yahweh is great in Zion; He is exalted above all the peoples. Let them praise Your great and awe-inspiring name. He is holy. (Ps. 99:1–3)

Surprisingly, during Jesus' earthy ministry, His disciples were not clear about these contrasts. As a result, they played regular rounds of "Who's the Greatest Disciple?"

Then they came to Capernaum. When He was in the house, He asked them, "What were you arguing about on the way?" But they were silent, because on the way they had been arguing with one another about who was the greatest. (Mark 9:33–34)

Living in God's Word, reading, studying, meditating on it, and memorizing it helps us put life into perspective. On our own merits, we are insignificant. Yet the great God of the Bible has revealed His love for us. God's perfection. Our sin. What a contrast.

Day 4

Everlasting

Your righteousness is an everlasting righteousness, and Your instruction is true. (Ps. 119:142)

Left to our own musing, we struggle with the concept of "everlasting." Anything that began infinitely in the past and extends infinitely into the future twists our minds like pretzels. Because God is everlasting, every attribute of God is infinite—His dominion, His covenants, His salvation, His love, and His righteousness.

The prophet Daniel recorded the confession of the powerful king of Babylon, Nebuchadnezzar, who experienced God in blessing and judgment.

But at the end of those days, I, Nebuchadnezzar, looked up to heaven, and my sanity returned to me. Then I praised the Most High and honored and glorified Him who lives forever: For His dominion is an everlasting dominion, and His kingdom is from generation to generation. All the inhabitants of the earth are counted as nothing, and He does what He wants with the army of heaven and the inhabitants of the earth. There is no one who can hold back His hand or say to Him, "What have You done?" (Dan. 4:34–35)

In a vision, Daniel saw the end of time and caught a glimpse of the God of eternity.

I continued watching in the night visions, and I saw One like a son of man coming with the clouds of heaven. He approached the Ancient of Days and was escorted before Him. He was given authority to rule, and glory, and a kingdom; so that those of every people, nation, and language should serve Him. His dominion is an everlasting dominion that will not pass away, and His kingdom is one that will not be destroyed. (Dan. 7:13–14)

As God's creation, we live as finite people preparing to transition into eternity. There we will experience God's everlasting attributes, His love or His judgment. God has given us His instruction so that we can know the truth, confess our sins, and cry out to God to be saved. Then we can face an everlasting future with the infinite God with humble confidence.

Day 5

Overtaken

Trouble and distress have overtaken me, but Your commands are my delight. Your decrees are righteous forever. Give me understanding, and I will live. (Ps. 119:143–144)

Running from trouble and distress, we struggle and stumble. Our pace slows, and the things we fear envelop us in a dust storm of darkness. We can identify with Job.

For the thing I feared has overtaken me, and what I dreaded has happened to me. (Job 3:25)

When life overtakes us, God's presence through His Word become increasingly delightful. We draw hope from passages that promise God's blessings to those who follow His Word.

"Now if you faithfully obey the LORD your God and are careful to follow all His commands I am giving you today, the LORD your God will put you far above all the nations of the earth. All these blessings will come and overtake you, because you obey the LORD your God: You will be blessed in the city and blessed in the country. Your descendants will be

blessed, and your land's produce, and the offspring of your livestock, including the young of your herds and the newborn of your flocks. Your basket and kneading bowl will be blessed. You will be blessed when you come in and blessed when you go out." (Deut. 28:1–6)

God is not a vending machine. We don't drop obedience in the slot, hit a button, and wait for blessings to pop out. But when troubles overtake us, we steady our hearts through faith. The book of Revelation describes the battles to come and the ultimate victory of Christ.

These will make war against the Lamb, but the Lamb will conquer them because He is Lord of lords and King of kings. Those with Him are called, chosen, and faithful." (Rev. 17:14)

All that can overtake us now, Christ has already conquered. We experience pain in the moment but will stand in victory for eternity.

Everlasting Righteousness
Psalm 119:137–144

Verse 1

You are righteous LORD and Your judgments are just.
Decrees You issue are righteous,
 and altogether trustworthy. My anger overwhelms me,
because my foes forget Your words.

Chorus

Your righteousness is an everlasting righteousness.
Your instruction is; it is true.

Trouble and distress have overtaken me, but Your commands are my delight.

Your righteousness is an everlasting righteousness.

Verse 2

Your word is completely pure,
and Your servant loves it.
I'm insignificant and despised,
but I don't forget Your precepts.

Repeat Chorus

Bridge

Your decrees are righteous; they are righteous forever.
Give me understanding, understanding and I will live.

Repeat Chorus and Close

Your righteousness is an everlasting righteousness.
Your instruction is; it is true.
Trouble and distress have overtaken me, but Your commands are my delight.
Your righteousness is an everlasting righteousness.
An everlasting righteousness.

Chapter 19

I Put My Hope in Your Word

I call with all my heart; answer me, LORD. I will obey Your statutes.

I call to You; save me, and I will keep Your decrees.

I rise before dawn and cry out for help; I put my hope in Your word.

I am awake through each watch of the night to meditate on Your promise.

In keeping with Your faithful love, hear my voice. LORD, give me life, in keeping with Your justice.

Those who pursue evil plans come near; they are far from Your instruction.

You are near, LORD, and all Your commands are true.

Long ago I learned from Your decrees that You have established them forever.

—Psalm 119:145–152

Day 1

Answer

I call with all my heart; answer me, LORD. I will obey Your statutes. I call to You; save me, and I will keep Your decrees. (Ps. 119:145–146)

In response to a question, we expect an answer. Sometimes the answer may be acknowledgment that the question has been heard. Usually, though, we want more than confirmation; we want content. We ask because we need something.

The prophet Jeremiah struggled to find the answers he needed from God. In response, God gave Him a promise that delights the asking heart.

Call to Me and I will answer you and tell you great and incomprehensible things you do not know. (Jer. 33:3)

In spite of God's great promises to answer, we puzzle at times over His timing. Like King David, we plead for a timely response in our time of need.

Don't hide Your face from Your servant, for I am in distress. Answer me quickly! (Ps. 69:17)

The psalmist focused on obeying God's statutes and keeping His decrees. In the same way, we pray on the basis of God's Word. Only then can our requests align with God's will. But what about those times when we face threatening circumstances and do not know God's will? Even then we can pray for God's favor.

But as for me, LORD, my prayer to You is for a time of favor. In Your abundant, faithful love, God, answer me with Your sure salvation. (Ps. 69:13)

God knows our needs, yet requires us to pray. We struggle with any delay to His answers. One day that will change. The prophet Isaiah glimpsed a future without delays.

Even before they call, I will answer; while they are still speaking, I will hear. (Isa. 65:24)

Until then, we pray, confident that God hears and always answers—yes, no, or not yet.

Day 2

Help

I rise before dawn and cry out for help; I put my hope in Your word. I am awake through each watch of the night to meditate on Your promise. (Ps. 119:147–148)

At times we ask God for specific things based on needs we face. At other times so much confronts us we don't know how to pray. Speaking the long list of all we need God to do feels overwhelming. God understands our wordless frailty, especially in times of sleepless fatigue. He accepts a powerful one-word prayer—"Help!"

Praying for help may sound inadequate. It's actually a powerful prayer with solid content. A prayer for help acknowledges what is lacking. We need assistance, aid, or support. Life presses us down, so we need relief. Praying specific prayers remains optimum, but in a crisis God will not ignore an urgent cry for "Help!"

King David is known for his elegant prayers. We can learn from his example. But we can also study his prayers for help, one of the most common elements of his prayers.

For He has not despised or detested the torment of the afflicted. He did not hide His face from him but listened when he cried to Him for help. (Ps. 22:24)

In my alarm I had said, "I am cut off from Your sight." But You heard the sound of my pleading when I cried to You for help. (Ps. 31:22)

David was a man after God's own heart, so he had a strong basis for prayer. Incredible but true, we have greater spiritual assets available to us in Christ as we pray.

In the same way the Spirit also joins to help in our weakness, because we do not know what to pray for as we should, but the Spirit Himself intercedes for us with unspoken groanings. (Rom. 8:26)

The Holy Spirit gathers up our inarticulate cries and transforms our feeble words into divine intercession acceptable to the Father. In response, God answers, helping us in our weakness. In those times when we don't know what to pray, we can mumble, "Help" with hope.

Day 3

Keeping

In keeping with Your faithful love, hear my voice. LORD, give me life, in keeping with Your justice. Those who pursue evil plans come near; they are far from Your instruction. (Ps. 119:149–150)

Imagine a street running through rows of modest ranch-style homes. Among them, though, stands one gaudy mansion stretched over five lots with Grecian statues and fountains.

We would wonder about those who built that house because it was not "in keeping" with the neighborhood.

When we pray, we ask God to take actions that are consistent with His character, His attributes, and His will as revealed in the Bible. That's why the psalmist could pray that God would hear "in keeping with your faithful love" or "in keeping with your justice." Never expect an answer to prayer that is not "in keeping" with the truth about God.

King David often framed his prayers in the context of what would be "in keeping" with God—His love, righteousness, and compassion.

Do not remember the sins of my youth or my acts of rebellion; in keeping with Your faithful love, remember me because of Your goodness, LORD. (Ps. 25:7)

Vindicate me, LORD my God, in keeping with Your righteousness, and do not let them rejoice over me. (Ps. 35:24)

Answer me, LORD, for Your faithful love is good; in keeping with Your great compassion, turn to me. (Ps. 69:16)

For the same reason, we can ask God to deal with those who pursue evil plans or those who are far from His instruction. They are doing things that are not "in keeping" with God's character or His will, so we have a strong basis for our requests.

The key to prayer is learning enough about God through His Word to pray for what aligns with His will and against what deviates from His will. That's why Jesus taught us to pray alignment prayers—for God's will be done on earth as it is in heaven.

Day 4

Near

You are near, LORD, and all Your commands are true. (Ps. 119:151)

Saying, "God is near" is simple. Grasping the implications of that statement exceeds our intellectual capabilities. The Bible tells the story of how people who were far from God could be brought near. The apostle Paul summarizes what made this possible:

But now in Christ Jesus, you who were far away have been brought near by the blood of the Messiah. (Eph. 2:13)

When the Messiah came, He proclaimed the good news of peace to you who were far away and peace to those who were near. For through Him we both have access by one Spirit to the Father. (Eph. 2:17–18)

The Law made people aware that they were far from God. It could not, however, keep them near to God. What a contrast to the hope we now have in Christ.

So the previous command is annulled because it was weak and unprofitable (for the law perfected nothing), but a better hope is introduced, through which we draw near to God. (Heb. 7:18–19)

Let us draw near with a true heart in full assurance of faith, our hearts sprinkled clean from an evil conscience and our bodies washed in pure water. (Heb. 10:22)

So how can we live in the reality of being near to God? Humble submission.

Draw near to God, and He will draw near to you. Cleanse your hands, sinners, and purify your hearts, double-minded people! Be miserable and mourn and weep. Your laughter must change to mourning and your joy to sorrow. Humble yourselves before the Lord, and He will exalt you. (James 4:8–10)

Old Testament saints experienced nearness to God as they obeyed God's Word and turned to Him by faith. That's why the psalmist could say, "You are near, Lord." But in Christ, we are always near God, not through our merit, but because of the price Jesus paid for our access.

Day 5

Established

Long ago I learned from Your decrees that You have established them forever. (Ps. 119:152)

Our world wobbles; at least that's how we perceive it. Nothing feels firmly in place or on a stable foundation. Our perception is wrong. The prophet Jeremiah corrects our thinking:

He made the earth by His power, established the world by His wisdom, and spread out the heavens by His understanding. (Jer. 51:15)

God created the world and holds it in place. He rules the world as our sovereign judge.

The LORD has established His throne in heaven, and His kingdom rules over all. (Ps. 103:19)

As evidence of His rule, God gave us His Word, first to Israel—commands, judgments, decrees, statutes, and laws that reflected His perfect character and righteous requirements.

These are the statutes, ordinances, and laws the LORD established between Himself and the Israelites through Moses on Mount Sinai. (Lev. 26:46)

All that God spoke in the past, He fulfilled in Christ through an everlasting covenant.

As they were eating, Jesus took bread, blessed and broke it, gave it to the disciples, and said "Take and eat it; this is My body." Then He took a cup, and after giving thanks, He gave it to them and said, "Drink from it, all of you. For this is My blood that establishes the covenant; it is shed for many for the forgiveness of sins." (Matt. 26:26–28)

Now we have the great privilege of being part of all that God has established, including His work of salvation in our lives.

Therefore, as you have received Christ Jesus the Lord, walk in Him, rooted and built up in Him and established in the faith, just as you were taught, overflowing with gratitude. (Col. 2:6–7)

Even when our lives shake, we turn through faith to the One who holds everything in its place.

I Put My Hope in Your Word
Psalm 119:145–152

Verse 1

I call with all my heart; answer me LORD, and I'll obey Your statutes.

I call to You. Save me, and I will keep Your decrees.

Chorus

I rise before dawn, and I cry out for help. I put my hope in Your word.

I am awake through each watch of the night to meditate on Your promise.

In keeping with Your faithful love, hear my voice.

I put my hope in Your word.

Verse 2

Give me life, O LORD, in keeping with Your justice.

Those who pursue evil plans come near. They are far from Your instruction.

Repeat Chorus

Bridge

You are near, LORD, and all Your commands are true.

Long ago I learned from Your decrees that You have established them forever.

Repeat Chorus and Close

I rise before dawn, and I cry for help. I put my hope in Your word.

I am awake through each watch of the night to meditate on Your promise.

In keeping with Your faithful love, hear my voice.

I put my hope in Your word. I put my hope in Your word.

I put my hope in Your word.

Chapter 20

Consider How I Love Your Precepts

Consider my affliction and rescue me, for I have not forgotten Your instruction.

Defend my cause, and redeem me; give me life, as You promised.

Salvation is far from the wicked because they do not seek Your statutes.

Your compassions are many, LORD; give me life, according to Your judgments.

My persecutors and foes are many. I have not turned from Your decrees.

I have seen the disloyal and feel disgust because they do not keep Your word.

Consider how I love Your precepts; LORD, give me life, according to Your faithful love.

The entirety of Your word is truth, and all Your righteous judgments endure forever.

—Psalm 119:153–160

Day 1

Rescue

Consider my affliction and rescue me, for I have not forgotten Your instruction. Defend my cause, and redeem me; give me life, as You promised. (Ps. 119:153–154)

A rescue requires one in need and one willing and able to help. The Bible presents us as the ones in need and God as the rescuer. The psalmist understood this reality. His affliction exceeded his ability to help himself, so he called on God.

During the time of the exile, the King of Babylon, Nebuchadnezzar, ordered everyone to fall down and worship a large, golden statue at appointed times. Failure to comply resulted in death in a fiery furnace. Three young Jews—Shadrach, Meshach, and Abednego—refused to bow and were brought before the king. Notice how they responded to the threat to their lives:

"If the God we serve exists, then He can rescue us from the furnace of blazing fire, and He can rescue us from the power of you, the king. But even if He does not rescue us, we want you as king to know that we will not serve your gods or worship the gold statue you set up." (Dan. 3:17–18)

What courage. They affirmed that their God could rescue them without presuming that He would. Even if God failed to intervene, they would not bow down. In a rage, the king commanded them thrown into the fire. When the king looked in, he was shocked.

He exclaimed, "Look! I see four men, not tied, walking around in the fire unharmed; and the fourth looks like a son of the gods." (Dan. 3:25)

When the three men walked out of the fire unhurt, Nebuchadnezzar marveled.

Nebuchadnezzar exclaimed, "Praise to the God of Shadrach, Meshach, and Abednego! He sent His angel and rescued His servants who trusted in Him." (Dan. 3:28)

In the same way, we testify that God has rescued us in Christ. He was able and willing.

He has rescued us from the domain of darkness and transferred us into the kingdom of the Son He loves. (Col. 1:13)

Day 2

Far

Salvation is far from the wicked because they do not seek Your statutes. (Ps. 119:155)

In spiritual matters, people can be far and near at the same time.

Throughout His earthy ministry, Jesus exhorted the Pharisees and other religious leaders. Confronted with the truth Jesus taught, they resisted, preferring their own rules and standards. Though near to Jesus physically, they remained far from salvation.

He answered them, "Isaiah prophesied correctly about you hypocrites, as it is written: These people honor Me with their lips, but their heart is far from Me. They worship Me in vain, teaching as doctrines the commands of men." (Mark 7:6–7)

Perhaps these leaders simply needed something clearer and more compelling, like seeing someone rise from the dead? In time, they had a front-row seat.

After He said this, He shouted with a loud voice, "Lazarus, come out!" The dead man came out bound hand and foot with linen strips and with his face wrapped in a cloth. Jesus said to them, "Loose him and let him go." (John 11:43–44)

Incredible but true, that miracle fortified the opposition. The religious leaders left Lazarus's empty tomb and plotted to kill Jesus. What they did not know was that their evil action was the key to God's eternal plan of salvation.

But now in Christ Jesus, you who were far away have been brought near by the blood of the Messiah. (Eph. 2:13)

Salvation remains impossibly far from all of us apart from God's grace. God's Word reveals the way to peace for all who will call on the name of the Lord.

When the Messiah came, He proclaimed the good news of peace to you who were far away and peace to those who were near. (Eph. 2:17)

Through the cross and resurrection of Jesus, those who were impossibly far from God have been brought incredibly near.

Day 3

Judgments

Your compassions are many, LORD; give me life, according to Your judgments. (Ps. 119:156)

As the righteous judge, God issues judgments—verdicts, sentences, and penalties. The Bible contains God's record of judgments throughout history and prophecies about what He will do in the future. Fortunately, God is a compassionate judge, as He explained to Moses:

Then the LORD passed in front of him [Moses] and proclaimed: Yahweh—Yahweh is a compassionate and gracious God, slow to anger and rich in faithful love and truth, maintaining faithful love to a thousand generations, forgiving wrongdoing, rebellion, and sin. But He will not leave the guilty unpunished. (Exod. 34:6–7)

When the priests moved the Ark into the place prepared for it, King David led the people in a prayer of thanksgiving that focused on God's work in the world and His judgments.

Search for the LORD and for His strength; seek His face always. Remember the wonderful works He has done, His wonders, and the judgments He has pronounced, you offspring of Israel His servant, Jacob's descendants—His chosen ones. He is the LORD our God; His judgments govern the whole earth. (1 Chron. 16:11–14)

Years later, after the death and resurrection of Jesus, the apostle Paul marveled at God, at His ways, His wisdom, and His judgments.

Oh, the depth of the riches both of the wisdom and the knowledge of God! How unsearchable His judgments and untraceable His ways! For who has known the mind of the Lord? Or who has been His counselor? Or who has ever first given to Him, and has to be repaid? For from Him and through Him and to Him are all things. To Him be the glory forever. Amen. (Rom. 11:33–36)

With the psalmist, we thank God for His compassions and humbly acknowledge the life He made possible for us as explained in His Word.

Day 4

Persecutors

My persecutors and foes are many. I have not turned from Your decrees. I have seen the disloyal and feel disgust because they do not keep Your word. (Ps. 119:157–158)

The Bible records the stories of many godly people who suffered, but it's hard to find one who suffered more than the prophet Jeremiah. Throughout his long ministry as Judah imploded, Jeremiah faced nothing but opposition. As he spoke God's truth to the people faithfully, they responded by mocking him, placing him in stocks, throwing him in a muddy cistern, and into prison. Like the psalmist, Jeremiah recoiled from the people's callous resistance to God and His Word. He called out to God continuously for help.

You know, LORD; remember me and take note of me. Avenge me against my persecutors. In Your patience, don't take me away. Know that I suffer disgrace for Your honor. (Jer. 15:15)

Faced with unrelenting opposition, Jeremiah prayed specific prayers for help.

Let my persecutors be put to shame, but don't let me be put to shame. Let them be terrified, but don't let me be terrified. Bring on them the day of disaster; shatter them with total destruction. (Jer. 17:18)

Even though God did not remove Jeremiah from his difficult assignment, Jeremiah continued to pray with faith, believing that God would vindicate him in time.

But the LORD is with me like a violent warrior. Therefore, my persecutors will stumble and not prevail. Since they have not succeeded, they will be utterly shamed, an everlasting humiliation that will never be forgotten. (Jer. 20:11)

When we build our lives on the truths in God's Word, persecutors do not surprise us. The harder they come at us, the stronger we cling to God's decrees. Opposition fortifies our resolve and clarifies the difference between our foes and us. So we join the psalmist, Jeremiah, and a long line who withstood persecutors because of God's call on their lives.

Day 5

Entirety

Consider how I love Your precepts; LORD, give me life, according to Your faithful love. The entirety of Your word is truth, and all Your righteous judgments endure forever. (Ps. 119:159–160)

What is true? Is there absolute truth? The debate rages today but is not new. Pontius Pilate raised this issue when he interrogated Jesus.

"You are a king then?" Pilate asked. "You say that I'm a king," Jesus replied. "I was born for this, and I have come into the world for this: to testify to the truth. Everyone who is of the truth listens to My voice." "What is truth?" said Pilate. After he had said this, he went out to the Jews again and told them, "I find no grounds for charging Him." (John 18:37–38)

Throughout His ministry, Jesus affirmed that He told people the truth. More important, He embodied truth.

Jesus told him, "I am the way, the truth, and the life. No one comes to the Father except through Me." (John 14:6)

While Jesus was "the truth," He pointed people to the truth in the Scriptures. We see this clearly when the Sadducees tried to trap Jesus with a question about the resurrection.

Jesus answered them, "You are deceived, because you don't know the Scriptures or the power of God." (Matt. 22:29)

The psalmist lived his life on the basis of God's Word. It is clear that he believed all the Scriptures were true—the laws, precepts, statutes, instructions, commands, teaching, judgments, ordinances, promises, and every other part. He loved God's Word and trusted God to give Him life through it. He believed God's Word would endure; it was not constrained by time and culture; it was binding on all people in every place in every age in history.

Pilate asked the right question. Unfortunately, he missed Jesus, the answer to His question. The entirety of God's Word is true. The truth is Jesus.

Consider How I Love Your Precepts
Psalm 119:153–160

Verse 1

Consider my affliction and rescue me, for I have not forgotten Your instruction.

Defend my cause, and redeem me. Give me life as You promised.

Chorus

Consider how I love Your precepts, Lord. Give me life according to Your faithful love.

The entirety of Your word is truth, and all Your righteous judgments

Endure forever, endure forever, endure forever.

Verse 2

Salvation is far from the wicked because they don't seek Your statutes.

Your compassions are many, LORD. Give me life, according to Your judgments.

Repeat Chorus

Bridge

My persecutors and foes are many,

But I have not turned from Your decrees.

I've seen the disloyal and feel disgust.

They do not keep Your word, Your word.

Repeat Chorus and Close

Consider how I love Your precepts, LORD. Give me life according to Your faithful love.

The entirety of Your word is truth, and all Your righteous judgments

Endure forever, endure forever, endure forever.

Chapter 21

Abundant Peace

Princes have persecuted me without cause, but my heart fears only Your word.

I rejoice over Your promise like one who finds vast treasure.

I hate and abhor falsehood, but I love Your instruction.

I praise You seven times a day for Your righteous judgments.

Abundant peace belongs to those who love Your instruction; nothing makes them stumble.

LORD, I hope for Your salvation and carry out Your commands.

I obey Your decrees and love them greatly.

I obey Your precepts and decrees, for all my ways are before You.

—Psalm 119:161–168

Day 1

Promise

Princes have persecuted me without cause, but my heart fears only Your word. I rejoice over Your promise like one who finds vast treasure. (Ps. 119:161–162)

Like the psalmist, Simeon lived on God's promises. For years he waited in Jerusalem for the coming of the Lord's Messiah. A righteous and devout man, he looked expectantly. He noticed Joseph and Mary the day they brought Jesus to the temple to be dedicated according to the Law. Imagine how the new parents felt as this old man asked to hold their baby and then launched into this public prayer of praise.

Guided by the Spirit, he entered the temple complex. When the parents brought in the child Jesus to perform for Him what was customary under the law, Simeon took Him up in his arms, praised God, and said: Now, Master, You can dismiss Your slave in peace, as You promised. For my eyes have seen Your salvation. You have prepared it in the presence of all peoples—a light for revelation to the Gentiles and glory to Your people Israel. Luke 2:27–32

Undoubtedly, people had taunted Simeon over the years for his dogged confidence in God's promise. But he did not falter, fearing only God and not men. That day, people saw what they expected to see. Most saw only a young couple with an ordinary baby. Simeon saw a long–promised treasure. Years later, Jesus would teach that the Kingdom of God was a treasure.

"The kingdom of heaven is like treasure, buried in a field, that a man found and reburied. Then in his joy he goes and sells everything he has and buys that field. Again, the kingdom of heaven is like a merchant in search of fine

pearls. When he found one priceless pearl, he went and sold everything he had, and bought it." (Matt. 13:44–46)

Never underestimate the value of God's promises. The psalmist didn't, and those promises sustained him; Simeon didn't, and he held God's promise in his arms.

Day 2

Falsehood

I hate and abhor falsehood, but I love Your instruction. I praise You seven times a day for Your righteous judgments. (Ps. 119:163–164)

When we love God's instruction, we can recognize what is false. Falsehood blankets the world with lies, like pine trees releasing spring pollen. Truth-lovers hate and abhor falsehood. Having discovered the truth, they regret every lie they believed and every avoidable consequence they endured. No wonder the psalmist praised God continually for His truth, His righteous judgments that revealed the crooked and twisted.

From the beginning, our world has hosted a cosmic contest between God's truth and Satan's lies. God's victory is assured, but Satan still plays out the game. It's no surprise that he twisted God's Word in the first temptation.

Now the serpent was the most cunning of all the wild animals that the LORD God had made. He said to the woman, "Did God really say, 'You can't eat from any tree in the garden'?" (Gen. 3:1)

The Bible says this pathetic game of lies will escalate until the end times when Satan will launch his goal- line stand of deception.

*The coming of the lawless one is based on Satan's working,
with all kinds of false miracles, signs, and wonders, and
with every unrighteous deception among those who are
perishing. They perish because they did not accept the love
of the truth in order to be saved. For this reason God sends
them a strong delusion so that they will believe what is false,
so that all will be condemned—those who did not believe the
truth but enjoyed unrighteousness. (2 Thess. 2:9–12)*

In the end, God allows people to have it their own way. If
they reject the truth and pursue the lie, God allows them to
catch the lie and eat its fruit. What an avoidable tragedy.

Day 3

Peace

*Abundant peace belongs to those who love Your instruction;
nothing makes them stumble. (Ps. 119:165)*

Oh, to find freedom from disturbance, quarrels, and dis-
agreement, a state of security, order, quiet, and tranquility.
Could we ever experience peace in abundance? Could peace
abound and overflow in our lives? To all of these, the psalmist
said, "Yes."

Peace is a by-product; part of a greater blessing instead
of something that stands alone. The Bible links our experience of peace to our relationship with the God of peace. The
apostle Paul explained the relationship in simple terms.

*May the Lord of peace Himself give you peace always in
every way. The Lord be with all of you. (2 Thess. 3:16)*

The obstacles to our peace with God stood impossibly high.
We could not positive-think or independently act our way out

of our brokenness. Those who claimed otherwise lied, as did the false prophets in the time of the prophet Jeremiah.

They have treated My people's brokenness superficially, claiming, "Peace, peace," when there is no peace. (Jer. 6:14)

The God of peace provided the way of peace through the cross of Christ. That's why Jesus could promise peace to His disciples.

"I have told you these things so that in Me you may have peace. You will have suffering in this world. Be courageous! I have conquered the world." (John 16:33)

Forget the quest for an obstacle-free life. Expect challenges, even suffering. All the while, rejoice that you have peace with God through Christ, then walk through life with the peace of His presence.

Do not seek peace. Walk in God's wisdom through God's Word. Focus on Jesus and find peace—abundant peace from the God of peace.

Day 4

Hope

LORD, *I hope for Your salvation and carry out Your commands. (Ps. 119:166)*

We cherish desires with anticipation, sensing what we want can happen. We hope.

Everyone hopes. The Bible draws a distinction, though, presenting hope as more than anticipatory longing. People of faith hope with confidence in God who controls all things, who creates out of nothing, speaking words and ideas into existence.

The object of hope determines the nature of hope. Left
to our own scheming, we could only long wistfully for salvation from the expanse of sin. No self-saving solution exists.
Drowning ones require intervention. Flailing helplessly, we
cry out for someone to pluck us out of danger. Life leaks
away as our lungs fill with hopelessness. Spewing out the vile
water of sin, we gasp and cough. But then a rescuer comes.
The infinitely strong lifts the incurably weak. The spotlight
of glory falls on the Savior, not the saved. So we cry out with
King David:

> You answer us in righteousness, with awe-inspiring works,
> God of our salvation, the hope of all the ends of the earth
> and of the distant seas. (Ps. 65:5)

God's Word reveals God's gift of salvation. In simple obedience, we do what God prescribes and receive the gift offered.

> If you confess with your mouth, "Jesus is Lord," and believe
> in your heart that God raised Him from the dead, you will
> be saved. (Rom. 10:9)

Having taken the most important step in life, we stand as
ones saved, those who can live with protective hope as the
apostle Paul described.

> But since we belong to the day, we must be serious and put
> the armor of faith and love on our chests, and put on a hel-
> met of the hope of salvation. (1 Thess. 5:8)

God's commands lead us to Christ, but then the confidence of salvation gives us a compelling desire to carry out
God's commands. The circle of hope is complete.

Day 5

Praying

I obey Your decrees and love them greatly. I obey Your precepts and decrees, for all my ways are before You. (Ps. 119:167–168)

Hezekiah, one of the kings of Israel, led Judah well. Although he was not perfect, he pursued God's ways and encouraged the people to return to God. Unfortunately, Hezekiah became ill with a terminal malady. In his distress, he prayed, begging God to heal him.

Then Hezekiah turned his face to the wall and prayed to the LORD. He said, "Please, LORD, remember how I have walked before You faithfully and wholeheartedly, and have done what pleases You." And Hezekiah wept bitterly. (Isa. 38:2–3)

Many pray for healing. God's criteria for responding remain shrouded in the mystery of His providence. To Hezekiah's prayer, God said, "Yes."

Then the word of the LORD came to Isaiah: "Go and tell Hezekiah that this is what the LORD God of your ancestor David says: I have heard your prayer; I have seen your tears. Look, I am going to add 15 years to your life." (Isa. 38:4–5)

In his prayer, Hezekiah acknowledges that his ways of living were before the Lord. He lived before an audience of One. So he pleaded with God for mercy. The quantity of Hezekiah's tears did not force God's positive response. God planned to use Hezekiah to advance the plans He had prophesied through Isaiah, so He extended Hezekiah's life fifteen years.

In the same way, the psalmist affirmed his love for God's decrees and precepts and his desire to obey them. He lived his life on stage before the Lord. Nothing was hidden; God saw everything—his love for God's Word and his desire to obey. This realization anchored the psalmist's life. He did not obey God to control God. He obeyed God because God was in control.

Our lives become unceasing prayers. What we do, think, and say reveal the depth to which God's Word has penetrated our hearts. We pray to please God. How we live reveals if we prayed or just talked to ourselves.

Abundant Peace
Psalm 11:161–168

Chorus

Abundant peace belongs to those who

love your instruction; nothing makes them stumble.

LORD I hope for your salvation and carry out Your commands.

Verse 1

Princes have persecuted me without cause, but my heart fears only Your word.

I rejoice over Your promise like one who finds vast treasure.

Repeat Chorus

Verse 2

I hate and abhor; I abhor falsehood,

but I love Your instruction.

I praise You seven times a day for Your righteous judgments.

Repeat Chorus then to Bridge

Bridge

I obey Your decrees and love them greatly.

I obey Your precepts and decrees,

for all my ways are,

All my ways are before you.

Repeat Chorus and Close

Abundant peace belongs to those who love your instruction; nothing makes them stumble.

LORD I hope for your salvation and carry out Your commands.

Carry out your commands. Carry out your commands.

Chapter 22

My Lips Pour Out Praise

Let my cry reach You, LORD; give me understanding according to Your word.

Let my plea reach You; rescue me according to Your promise.

My lips pour out praise, for You teach me Your statutes.

My tongue sings about Your promise, for all Your commandments are righteous.

May Your hand be ready to help me, for I have chosen Your precepts.

I long for Your salvation, LORD, and Your instruction is my delight.

Let me live, and I will praise You; may Your judgments help me.

I wander like a lost sheep; seek Your servant, for I do not forget Your commands.

—Psalm 119:169–176

Day 1

Plea

Let my cry reach You, LORD; give me understanding according to Your word. Let my plea reach You; rescue me according to Your promise. (Ps. 119:169–170)

Read these two sentences and think about the images that pop into your mind with both: "I heard him talking," or, "I heard him crying and pleading." Can you feel the intensity of the second one? Can you see the tears and hear the anguished voice? Crying and pleading evoke images of distress, of earnest requests for aid, and calls for immediate attention. At times, life prompts us to talk. At other times, life requires us to plead.

Throughout Psalm 119, the psalmist talked to God. In this case, distress overwhelmed him. Talking intensifies with urgency and tears, transforming words beyond mere communication into groans of the soul. King David often prayed with such intensity.

God, listen to my prayer and do not ignore my plea for help. Pay attention to me and answer me. I am restless and in turmoil with my complaint, because of the enemy's voice, because of the pressure of the wicked. For they bring down disaster on me and harass me in anger. (Ps. 55:1–3)

The pleading person lacks leverage. Everything rests with the one called upon. The psalmist asked for understanding based on God's Word. In the midst of his travail, he wanted to understand what was happening so he could pray the right way. He needed his cries and pleas to reach God, for only God could rescue him. Spiritual pilgrims traveling up to Jerusalem spoke to God with the same urgency.

Out of the depths I call to You, Yahweh! Lord, listen to my voice; let Your ears be attentive to my cry for help. (Ps. 130:1–2)

If we understood the depth of our needs and grasped the abundance of God's power and mercy, we would transform our prayers. Mindless streams of words would become pleas focused on our only source of help.

Day 2

Praise

My lips pour out praise, for You teach me Your statutes. My tongue sings about Your promise, for all Your command- ments are righteous. (Ps. 119:171–172)

Only God can transform pleading into praise and cries into song.

May the LORD be praised, for He has heard the sound of my pleading. The LORD is my strength and my shield; my heart trusts in Him, and I am helped. Therefore my heart rejoices, and I praise Him with my song. (Ps. 28:6–7)

Through His Word, God teaches us His statutes, His promises, and His commandments. As a result, we focus on Him with full confidence during our distress. Often our circumstances overwhelm us. Failing to see a way forward, we slip into despair. The enemy of our souls whispers lies. To fight back, we speak God's truth to our hearts. Like a prosecuting attorney, we build a case against depression and turmoil. We demand our hearts acknowledge the truth so that we adjust our actions.

Why am I so depressed? Why this turmoil within me? Put your hope in God, for I will still praise Him, my Savior and my God. (Ps. 42:11)

The words of Psalm 119 drill into our minds, reprograming our thinking with spiritual realities. Couple these words with music, and truth envelops us in a greenhouse of praise. The context of our lives changes even if the circumstances of our lives do not. Fortified with God's perspective, we decide to praise, to agree with God in spite of how we feel, and affirm what God calls "true" no matter what we see.

God deserves substantive praise, not spiritual pablum. True praise requires praiseworthy truth. Truth requires revelation from God. So when we praise God, we rehearse what God has told us in His Word and then speak and sing God's Word back to Him. A supremely righteous God deserves distinctive praise, not spiritual–sounding ditties pitched heavenward with careless distraction. God gives us truth; we echo that truth through praise.

Day 3

Ready

May Your hand be ready to help me, for I have chosen Your precepts. (Ps. 119:173)

The fractured human soul trends toward independence. Given a choice, we do things ourselves. Control feels better than admitting limitations. Only when pushed will we admit that we need help. Reality, though, rebuts our illusion of self-sufficiency. In fact, we need help often. Why? Because God designed us for dependence, not independence.

Jesus' mission on earth was infinitely complex. As God, He limited Himself to live as man. While His critics chaffed at

His claims to be God, they stared slack-jawed as He explained His relationship to His heavenly Father as man.

> *Then Jesus replied, "I assure you: The Son is not able to do anything on His own, but only what He sees the Father doing. For whatever the Father does, the Son also does these things in the same way. For the Father loves the Son and shows Him everything He is doing, and He will show Him greater works than these so that you will be amazed. (John 5:19–20)*

As the perfect man, Jesus knew what we struggle to admit—man's constant need for God. Never acting independently, Jesus lived with constant dependence on His Father. In the process, Jesus revealed God to us. In addition, He revealed "man" to us, showing us how we should live. Jesus explained to His disciples why their future would improve once He returned to the Father.

> *"I assure you: The one who believes in Me will also do the works that I do. And he will do even greater works than these, because I am going to the Father." (John 14:12)*

By design, God stands ready to help us. He works through those who rely on Him in faith, empowering those whose lives align with His will expressed through His Word. Our needs push us to God in utter dependence so we live as God intended, relying on Him. Our constant need intercepts God's readiness to help us just as Jesus demonstrated.

Day 4

Delight

I long for Your salvation, LORD, and Your instruction is my delight. Let me live, and I will praise You; may Your judgments help me. (Ps. 119:174–175)

Our longings and delights propel our lives. Unfortunately, we often delight in the wrong things. The apostle James explained this problem:

What is the source of wars and fights among you? Don't they come from the cravings that are at war within you? You desire and do not have. You murder and covet and cannot obtain. You fight and war. You do not have because you do not ask. You ask and don't receive because you ask with wrong motives, so that you may spend it on your evil desires. (James 4:1–3)

The battle James described rages in our hearts, creating conflict and discontent. Our evil desires drive us away from God's perfect purpose for us. Rather than implementing a "desire management" program, we need new desires. Instead of striving for incremental improvements in our "wants," we need new hearts that want the right things. One psalmist explained the process this way:

Take delight in the LORD, and He will give you your heart's desires. (Ps. 37:4)

Don't think this verse provides a fail-proof system to coerce God to give us what we desire. As we delight in the Lord, experiencing great pleasure and supreme satisfaction in Him, God performs a miracle. Rather than giving us what we want, God changes what we want. God's salvation, now and in eternity, dominates our thinking. God's instruction cheers our souls with divine truth. With a transformed perspective, the things in our lives, not just the good but the hard, become fodder for praise. Life never becomes easy, but God's Word reframes our circumstances. We desire God, trusting that whatever He allows to intercept our lives, He uses for our good within His grand purpose.

Day 5

Lost

I wander like a lost sheep; seek Your servant, for I do not forget Your commands. (Ps. 119:176)

Even with the compass of God's Word, we still get lost at times.

We all went astray like sheep; we all have turned to our own way. (Isa. 53:6)

Saying "I'm lost" sounds bad, but it's actually good. If you're lost, it means you're not where you belong. If you're lost, it implies that someone cares you are out of place. If you're lost, someone will search for you. The classification "lost" requires a reference point—a place to be and someone who cares. Lacking these, your situation may be sad, but you're not lost.

One of the great truths of the Bible is that God seeks the lost. He provides the reference point of where we should be, expresses concern for us, and launches the search. Jesus explained His mission on earth as a search.

"For the Son of Man has come to seek and to save the lost." (Luke 19:10)

Without God's commands, we would not know we are off track. Our self-programmed, internal gyroscopes would never detect our deviation from the divine plan. God proclaimed His love for the lost and the way He would express that love.

For God loved the world in this way: He gave His One and Only Son, so that everyone who believes in Him will not perish but have eternal life. (John 3:16)

God did not love us abstractly; He loved us specifically—sacrificing Jesus as the perfect payment for our sins. Only in this way could the lost be found, could enemies become friends. God overcame our wandering with His seeking, our displacement with access into His presence. Jesus became our searching shepherd, our sacrificing shepherd, and our infinitely good shepherd who laid down His life for us.

My Lips Pour Out Praise
Psalm 119:169–176

Verse 1

Let my cry reach You; give me understanding according to Your word.

Let my plea reach You; rescue me according to Your promise.

My lips pour out praise. My lips pour out praise.

Chorus

My lips pour out praise, for You teach me Your statutes.

My tongue sings about Your promise,

for all Your commandments are righteous.

May Your hand be ready to help me, for I have chosen Your precepts.

My lips pour out praise.

Verse 2

I long for Your salvation and Your instruction. Lord, it's my delight.

Let me live, and I will praise You; may Your judgments help me.

My lips pour out praise. My lips pour out praise.

Repeat Chorus

Bridge

I wander like a lost sheep; seek Your servant,

for I do not forget Your commands.

Repeat Chorus and Close

My lips pour out praise, for You teach me Your statutes.

My tongue sings about Your promise,

for all Your commandments are righteous.

May Your hand be ready to help me, for I have chosen Your precepts.

My lips pour out praise. My lips pour out praise. My lips pour out praise.

Your Lifelong Psalm 119 Experience

Did Psalm 119 draw you in? Do you think about God's Word differently as a result of your devotional journey? If so, keep moving forward.

Our relationship with God begins now and extends throughout eternity. Every investment we make in that relationship is valuable. Here are two practical steps for you to consider: accelerate your intake of God's Word and expand your praying using the pattern we find in Psalm 119.

More of God's Word

When you come to the end of your life, what will be your testimony of the impact of God's Word? It's clear the writer of Psalm 119 focused his life on God's Word, drawing on God's truth for everything he encountered. His experience should convict us because we have so much more of God's revelation. In our hands, we hold both testaments—Old and New. Rather than prophecies about the coming Messiah, we have full accounts of Jesus' life and the story of the early church. We could spend a lifetime and never exhaust what God has provided for us in the Bible. Pastor and writer John Stott once said, "God speaks through what He has spoken." Since that is true, how much of what God has spoken do we engage? Part of it? All of it? How often?

Many people find the Bible formidable. They want to read the entire Bible but fail to start or falter along the way. Knowing the Bible is deep they plan to read slowly, not moving on to new sections until they understand what they have just read. The problem, though, is that stopping at each verse you don't understand can prevent you from reading what comes next, something you will understand and desperately need.

So how about a radical suggestion? Rather than reading less of the Bible more slowly, consider reading more of the Bible rapidly. Here's how I stumbled onto this plan.

As part of my *Psalm 119 Experience*, I wanted to increase my personal Bible reading. I had read about spiritual leaders in past centuries that developed the discipline of reading through the Bible every year; some even read the entire Bible once every quarter. After assuming initially that there was no way I could do what they did, I decided to aim for once a quarter, without telling anyone, of course.

Using my online Bible study tool, *WordSearch*, I generated a customized reading plan. Fortunately, there are many tools available online these days to help. *WordSearch* worked great for me. I determined the time period I wanted to tackle, and the program generated my daily reading plan. To stay engaged as I read, I started my accelerated reading plan with an unmarked Bible. I didn't want anything to distract me, including old notes and underlines.

Remember, I determined to move fast; so after some trial and error, I discovered I do best with Bibles formatted with two columns on each page. With my colored pencil in hand, I moved quickly down the columns, marking as I went. If I saw something I didn't understand (that happened often), I put a question mark in a circle to the side of the verse.

Primarily, though, I focused on what I did understand. I was pleasantly surprised to discover that moving quickly through the Bible gave me a big-picture overview that helped me see how the Bible fit together.

Many publishers provide useful tools to help us read through the Bible in one year, providing a mix of Old Testament and New Testament every day. This is a great option. I discovered, however, great value in reading the Bible straight through because I sensed the longing in the Old Testament for Jesus' coming in the New Testament.

If you read straight through the Bible, you'll pick up a rhythm. No matter at what pace you move—twelve months, six months, or three months—you'll spend two-thirds of your time in the Old Testament and one-third in the New Testament.

One of the reasons I've enjoyed doing some ultrafast read-throughs, moving at the 3-month pace, is that I don't have to wait as long to get to the New Testament. Plus, I need more spiritual support than most people so I want to expose my mind and heart to as much of God's Word as possible on an ongoing basis. Inevitably, what I read in the sections each day address issues I faced that day. Perhaps because I read more of the Bible daily than I have done over the years, I experienced the "just in time" nature of God's Word more often.

I worried initially that I would not be able to read through the Bible consistently over a longer period of time. In previous years, I had attempted to read through the Bible and managed to do so but only by doing tedious "catch-up" blocks of reading when I missed a day (or a week, or longer).

One of the surprising things about doing a fast read through the Bible is that missing a day was not an option. Once behind, the gap multiplied too fast. Rather than discouraging me, I found this reality motivated me to set aside time to read every day.

Because I wanted to read a longer section of the Bible every day, I had to set aside specific time to do so. Having this priority helped me focus and make time for the spiritual race I wanted to run. At the same time, I gave myself "grace" if I faced a particularly challenging day when time was tight. When that happened, I raced through the assigned chapters, noting highlights as I went, but not lingering long.

Since I was not reading the Bible to impress anyone or to compete, I gave myself permission to never get behind. Every day, I completed the assigned chapters even if "complete" meant that on some days I really just scanned the text and circled a few passages.

I've always wanted to read the Bible all the way through in different translations. My accelerated reading program gave me the opportunity. Like many American Christians, I have multiple Bibles in various translations sitting on my shelves. Occasionally people would ask, "Have you read all those Bibles?" In the past, I would have replied honestly, "Of course not." But after several years of using my accelerated reading program, I've made great progress toward my goal. In fact, I now look forward to publishers releasing new translations.

Switching between different types of translations gave me variety. I enjoyed reading the King James Version (a first for me) as well as paraphrases and others versions with different translation philosophies. Looking at an unmarked page in a new translation helped keep my mind fresh as I read and held my attention.

The last thing I want to do is make you feel guilty or set you up for frustration. Remember that in the Christian life, our goal is to make progress from where we are . . . no matter how far along the path of discipleship we may be. You and I compete with no one. So start where you are and begin moving forward. Here are some incremental options.

- If you've never read a chapter of the Bible consistently, read Psalm 119 every day for thirty days and see what happens.
- If you've never read longer sections of the Bible, read Luke then Acts over thirty days and watch what God does in your life.
- If you've never read the entire New Testament, start out and read a few chapters a day until you work all the way through.
- If you've never read the entire Bible, try a "fast read" through the entire Bible, first on a twelve-month pace and then increasing speed over time.
- If you've read and studied the Bible for years, why not experiment with a three-month, rapid read-through just to see what happens. You may be surprised.

The writer of Psalm 119 wrote to encourage others to recognize the power and importance of God's Word. It makes sense that part of our lifelong *Psalm 119 Experience* would be accelerating our exposure to all that God has revealed in the Bible.

More Intention in Prayer

As a result of my *Psalm 119 Experience*, I became convicted (again) by my anemic prayer life. Over time, I've found myself driveling out prayers with the same old words, mindlessly speaking to God. Frankly, I became bored with the process at times. I shudder to think about God's response to my tired monologues.

The pattern used by the writer of Psalm 119 fascinated me. As we've seen, he structured his psalm with precision, writing eight lines that each began with the first letter of the alphabet, then eight lines with the next letter, all the way to eight lines with the last letter. We suspect his goal was to recall the psalm personally and to help others remember it. But was there more to it? As God worked through the psalmist to write what God intended, did the poetic structure of the psalm stretch the writer? How could it not?

After spending so much time with Psalm 119, I recognized that while the writer focused on God's Word, he actually wrote prayers. He didn't just write about God's Word; he prayed based on God's Word. The poetry shaped his praying. This realization launched an experiment for me—alphabet praying.

To force myself out of my prayer rut, I began a journal with twenty-six tabs, one for each letter in the English alphabet. Using a dictionary, I jotted down words under each tab to use in praying. The options for some letters run a bit slim, but I didn't give up. Not every day but as I could, I would turn to one of the letter tabs and write an eight-line prayer.

After struggling initially, I improved over time. I even eked out some "X" prayers (by bending the rules just a bit). No illusions of writing notable prayers or great poetry deterred me. I wasn't writing for other people. My goal was simple—I wanted to pray better, with more intention, replacing tired, retreaded words with fresh ones. The experiment engaged my mind and helped me pray with more confidence.

I didn't read my Psalm 119 prayers to God; I simply wrote them, considering them prayer-stretching exercises. I hoped my writing would strengthen my praying—not public praying, just my ongoing talks with God. The effort paid off. I remain frustrated with my prayer life and continue to ask God to teach me to pray. I do sense, however, that He is answering that prayer, in part, by pointing me to alphabet praying.

If you're frustrated with your prayer life, especially if you recycle the words in your prayers like sitcoms on cable, then give alphabet praying a try. I've included one example in the next chapter to help you get started. Hopefully, you'll discover new joy in prayer as I have by stretching your vocabulary of prayer and matching your praying with your accelerated exposure to God's Word.

The Unending Experience with God

God has given us all we need in Christ. He provided the way of salvation and gave us His Holy Spirit to live in us. Having begun new life in Christ, He calls us to live life with Him. We don't base our faith on experience. Like our feelings, our experiences will deceive and disappoint. But if we focus on God's Word, accelerating our exposure to the Bible while simultaneously expanding our praying to reflect God's truth with depth, we will experience God in new ways. The Christian life is a journey of devotion. Psalm 119 provides a guide for an adventure we will not forget.

An Alphabet Prayer

A

Almighty God, grant me worthy words of
adoration. Increase my spiritual vocabulary and
allow me to express fully my love for You.
Accept my faltering attempts to pray, this holy
activity with which I struggle. How I fail to
ascribe to You glory due. Though I try, all my
attempts fall short. I'm embarrassed and
admit my failure. O God, teach me to pray.

B

Be in thinking, O God, all that You are in fact.
Break through my small thoughts of You.
Beckon me to see more, experience more, to
behold You, not my image of You.
Begin again to stretch my mind to grasp more,
blessing me with your greatest gift—You.
Brighten my heart with the comfort of your presence,
bathing me in light, quenching all darkness.

C

Conflict rages in my soul, O God, yet You
constrain me in Your mercy. How can I
conceive my good fortune in Christ? You
conferred on me, your enemy, access as Your child.
Condemned before You in sin, I was helpless, yet Your
concern for me, expressed in the gospel, drew me,
compelled me. No merit exists in me. As I am, I
confess Christ, crowned, exalted above all.

D

Diminish the fear in my heart that
dulls faith and weighs me down. Let me not
demand an easier path before I will walk with
devotion. I long to fight with courage the
defeated enemy of my soul. Let his crafty ways
defraud me no longer. Let sin no longer
dull my love for You. I follow not out of
duty but with a profound sense of privilege.

E

Enough of casual discipleship, O Lord. I've
endured its withering force too long, failing to
enjoy all You have given while I seek other things.
Each day brings new opportunities and fresh resolve so
encourage my fractured soul—my mind, will, and
emotions, all that I am. Please be the cause of the
effect in my life. Change me. Empower me.
Energize me with the divine to live a holy life.

F

Focus my mind, Lord, on your promises,
freeing my heart to rest and not fear.
Friend of the weak, steady me now with
fortifying faith, Your initial and ongoing gift.
Foundation of my life, let me live for Your
fame, your renown. May I stand
firm, unmovable in Christ, walking, not
fainting, until I complete this earthy pilgrimage.

G

Grandeur and majesty, infinite holiness,
goodness and mercy draw me to You,

groaning with the magnitude of my sin yet
gaining Christ's perfect work on the cross.
Grip me with strong hands, O God. Place the .
goal of transformation in Christ as the
growing passion within me. Your wonderful
gift began this good work. Now complete it in Christ.

H

How can it be, Eternal God, that Your grace
has included me? My sin was
hideous, separating me from You. How
hopeless my task of earning right-standing with the
Holy. Nothing I could do would ever fill the
hole of sin in which I lived. Justice required
hell for me. Only Your great mercy
halted the sentence I deserved and heaped wrath on Jesus.

I

Instruct my mind and heart this day as I teach others.
Instill in me your wisdom so I may declare Your
incorruptible truth. How inadequate I feel. How
impossible this teacher's task of declaring Your mysteries.
Inevitably, I will misspeak. Protect my students, Great
   Teacher.
Intercede for me, Holy Spirit, that I may serve well.
Ignite the hearts of my students to burn as Your Word
intercepts their thoughts and leads them to You.

J

Jaunty, self-absorbed living has become a
jumbled, conflicted mass of dissatisfaction.
Juxtapose my fragmented life against
Jesus' integrated life of obedience.
Jolt me with the contrast. In my complacency,

jar me with a fresh vision of You, Your
justice and love resolved in a cross, theological
jazz, purposefully structured yet without constraint.

K

Knowing through Your self-revealing Word yet my
knowledge is incomplete. The mystery You unveil
keeps me probing to find out more. I pick at the
knot of divine truth that defies unraveling.
Kneeling, I acknowledge You are infinitely more,
kind to condescend to elemental explanations, offering
keys to unlock my understanding, leaving a
kaleidoscope of truth tumbling in beautiful combinations.

L

Listen, Loving Father, to my faltering words. I
lack the language to worship the
Lamb of God appropriately. Forgive my spiritual
laziness in prayer, the stale, hard
leftovers I give You—thoughts, words, and time.
Lift me up again so I will not
lapse into compromise and deadening
lethargy, hesitating to take up my cross and follow You.

M

Merge my rebellious will with Your perfect plans.
Mend my brokenness with your healing Word.
Map the story of your gracious work on my
mind until Your grand story becomes my
music, my song of praise. Take my hard heart and
melt it. Make me soft to your Spirit, never
marginal in my response, rather fast and full with
much joy as I flee sin and race to You.

N

Nothing could prepare me fully for this
next step of discipleship, this adventure, this
new opportunity to follow Jesus. Out of the
nest, uncertain, vulnerable, pushed out
nonetheless. Free falling, faltering flight,
navigating with eyes closed, sensing You
noiselessly hovering above, then below, always
near, bearing me upward on eagles' wings.

O

Orchestrate my day, O God, with new
opportunities to obey. Break down my
obstinate chaffing against the Spirit's prompting.
Once again, empower me for unbroken
obedience. Allow every trial to become an
occasion for faith, every step forward an
offering. Transform each measure of my life into an
overture of praise, O Conductor of my soul.

P

Paper with words, unique among all sacred texts,
powerful truth. O God, You speak now, clearly,
purposefully through what You have spoken.
Published on parchment and paper, these
prophetic words fulfilled in the Living Word.
Perfect wisdom, divine mystery, revealed to make
peace possible. The incredibly far brought impossibly near.
Prize of the ages, offered again to my dull heart.

Q

Quagmires of anxious thoughts breed
questions and fears, distracting, immobilizing.

Quivering in confusion, I stop, waiting,
quizzing in prayer to find direction, answers.
Quoting Scriptures, promises, anything to
quantify faith with divine facts. Give me
quarter in your presence until faith
quadruples and quintuples as I rely on You.

R

Rebuke those who wait for my fall,
reveling when I stumble, joking about my
regrets and resenting my progress. Grant me
resolve to pray for my persecutors, those who
rally against me, repeating lies and
replaying past failures for their gain to
restrict my future prospects. Forgive them, O God.
Refine me through these trials for Your glory.

S

Squeeze me, Lord, if required for change.
Spur me by your Spirit to move.
Stop me before sin lures me.
Surround me with spiritual protection.
Subsume my will in Yours.
Spark in me fresh devotion.
Sever my love for the world.
Showcase Jesus in my life.

T

Tether me, Lord, closely to you
today lest I slip. Empower me for
taut discipleship, no slack, no
tepid responses to Your revelation.
Take over my life and reign powerfully,
toppling all resistance and

transforming my tendencies so
they align thoroughly with Your will on earth.

U

Unable, I am. Omnipotent, You are.
Unclean, I am. Pure, You are.
Untenable, my sin. Unlimited Your provision.
Unpunished I stand before a cross-punished Christ.
Unblemished in the Beloved, redemption's mystery.
Unburdened now by Jesus' burden bearing.
Unceasing sanctification, rough but relentless.
Unashamed in allegiance to You, my Sovereign.

V

Veils removed. Access granted. Curtain torn
vertically from top to bottom, an invitation to
venture into the Holy—ultimate access
validated by the cross-paid price. Sin
vanquished by resurrection power; the
vacuum filled by Love's fullness. The law's standards
validated with perfect obedience. From defeat,
victory flowed in the triumphant Son.

W

Warn my soul constantly through your
Word of the folly of sin that sowing the
wind will reap the whirlwind. Holy Spirit,
work in me, reminding me of Your
ways through Your Word. Spare me the
wreckage of a life seduced by sin. Make me
wise enough to submit to Your truth revealed.
Wean me from the world so I long only for You.

X

Express salvation's music through me,
exquisite praise, clear tones. I'm a spiritual
xylophone designed for You to play.
Exude the clear tones of Your life with
excellence through my limitation, showing the
extravagance of your transforming power, the
expanse of Your mercy. Allow Your music to
expand in me until others see only You, Maestro.

Y

Yielding joyfully, I bow before You,
Yahweh—great God of covenant. In
Your infinite wisdom You uttered a divine
"Yes" that included me in salvation's plan. Now I
yearn to live out the implications of Your holiness,
yoked with Jesus. In my brokenness, I
yield to Your gracious guidance. An old life dead,
yet all things have burst forth new in You.

Z

Zap the chains, O God. Sin's
zoo has led me too long, a spiritual
zebra, black and white stripes
zipped over Your new creation. Give me
zeal to break free of the old skin,
zestfully stretching with expulsive power,
zooming forward with new life, a spiritual
zealot transfixed on Your glory now and forever.

The 22 Songs in the
Psalm 119 Experience

Song 1: Blameless Way

How happy are those whose way is blameless, who live according to law of the Lord! Happy are those who keep His decrees and seek Him with all their heart. They do nothing wrong; they follow His ways. You have commanded that Your precepts be diligently kept. If only my ways were committed to keeping Your statutes! Then I would not be ashamed when I think about all Your commands. I will praise You with a sincere heart when I learn Your righteous judgments. I will keep Your statutes; never abandon me. (Ps. 119:1–8)

Song 2: Pure Through God's Word

How can a young man keep his way pure? By keeping Your word. I have sought You with all my heart; don't let me wander from Your commands. I have treasured Your word in my heart so that I may not sin against You. LORD, may You be praised; teach me Your statutes. With my lips I proclaim all the judgments from Your mouth. I rejoice in the way revealed by Your decrees as much as in all riches. I will meditate on Your precepts and think about Your ways. I will delight in Your statutes; I will not forget Your word. (Ps. 119:9–16)

Song 3: Wonderful Things in Your Law

Deal generously with Your servant so that I might live; then I will keep Your word. Open my eyes so that I may see wonderful things in Your law. I am a stranger on earth; do not hide Your commands from me. I am continually overcome by longing for Your judgments. You rebuke the proud, the accursed, who wander from Your commands. Take insult and contempt away from me, for I have kept Your decrees. Though princes sit together speaking against me, Your servant will think about Your statutes; Your decrees are my delight and my counselors. (Ps. 119:17–24)

Song 4: Life Through Your Word

My life is down in the dust; give me life through Your word. I told You about my life, and You listened to me; teach me Your statutes. Help me understand the meaning of Your precepts so that I can meditate on Your wonders. I am weary from grief; strengthen me through Your word. Keep me from the way of deceit, and graciously give me Your instruction. I have chosen the way of truth; I have set Your ordinances before me. I cling to Your decrees; LORD, do not put me to shame. I pursue the way of Your commands, for You broaden my understanding. (Ps. 119:25–32)

Song 5: Give Me Life in Your Ways

Teach me, LORD, the meaning of Your statutes, and I will always keep them. Help me understand Your instruction, and I will obey it and follow it with all my heart. Help me stay on the path of Your commands, for I take pleasure in it. Turn my heart to Your decrees and not to material gain. Turn my eyes from looking at what is worthless; give me life in Your ways. Confirm what You said to Your servant, for it produces reverence for You. Turn away the disgrace I dread; indeed, Your judgments are good. How I long for Your precepts! Give me life through Your righteousness. (Ps. 119:33–40)

Song 6: Never Take the Word

Let Your faithful love come to me, LORD, Your salvation, as You promised. Then I can answer the one who taunts me, for I trust in Your word. Never take the word of truth from my mouth, for I hope in Your judgments. I will always keep Your law, forever and ever. I will walk freely in an open place because I seek Your precepts. I will speak of Your decrees before kings and not be ashamed. I delight in Your commands, which I love. I will lift up my hands to Your commands, which I love, and will meditate on Your statutes. (Ps. 119:41–48)

Song 7: Your Statutes

Remember Your word to Your servant; You have given me hope through it. This is my comfort in my affliction: Your promise has given me life. The arrogant constantly ridicule me, but I do not turn away from Your instruction. LORD, I remember Your judgments from long ago and find comfort. Rage seizes me because of the wicked who reject Your instruction. Your statutes are the theme of my song during my earthly life. I remember Your name in the night, LORD, and I keep Your law. This is my practice: I obey Your precepts. (Ps. 119:49–56)

Song 8: Hurried, Not Hesitating

The LORD is my portion; I have promised to keep Your words. I have sought Your favor with all my heart; be gracious to me according to Your promise. I thought about my ways and turned my steps back to Your decrees. I hurried, not hesitating to keep Your commands. Though the ropes of the wicked were wrapped around me, I did not forget Your law. I rise at midnight to thank You for Your righteous judgments. I am a friend to all who fear You, to those who keep Your precepts. LORD, the earth is filled with Your faithful love; teach me Your statutes. (Ps. 119:57–64)

Song 9: You're Good

LORD, You have treated Your servant well, just as You promised. Teach me good judgment and discernment, for I rely on

Your commands. Before I was afflicted I went astray, but now I keep Your word. You are good, and You do what is good; teach me Your statutes. The arrogant have smeared me with lies, but I obey Your precepts with all my heart. Their hearts are hard and insensitive, but I delight in Your instruction. It was good for me to be afflicted so that I could learn Your statutes. Instruction from Your lips is better for me than thousands of gold and silver pieces. (Ps. 119:65–72)

Song 10: Faithful Love

Your hands made me and formed me; give me understanding so that I can learn Your commands. Those who fear You will see me and rejoice, for I put my hope in Your word. I know, LORD, that Your judgments are just and that You have afflicted me fairly. May Your faithful love comfort me as You promised Your servant. May Your compassion come to me so that I may live, for Your instruction is my delight. Let the arrogant be put to shame for slandering me with lies; I will meditate on Your precepts. Let those who fear You, those who know Your decrees, turn to me. May my heart be blameless regarding Your statutes so that I will not be put to shame. (Ps. 119:73–80)

Song 11: How Many Days

I long for Your salvation; I put my hope in Your word. My eyes grow weary looking for what You have promised; I ask, "When will You comfort me?" Though I have become like a wineskin dried by smoke, I do not forget Your statutes. How many days must Your servant wait? When will You execute judgment on my persecutors? The arrogant have dug pits for me; they violate Your instruction. All Your commands are true; people persecute me with lies—help me! They almost ended my life on earth, but I did not abandon Your precepts.

Give me life in accordance with Your faithful love, and I will obey the decree You have spoken. (Ps. 119:81–88)

Song 12: Lord, Your Word Is Forever

LORD, Your word is forever; it is firmly fixed in heaven. Your faithfulness is for all generations; You established the earth, and it stands firm. They stand today in accordance with Your judgments, for all things are Your servants. If Your instruction had not been my delight, I would have died in my affliction. I will never forget Your precepts, for You have given me life through them. I am Yours; save me, for I have sought Your precepts. The wicked hope to destroy me, but I contemplate Your decrees. I have seen a limit to all perfection, but Your command is without limit. (Ps. 119:89–96)

Song 13: How Sweet Your Word

How I love Your teaching! It is my meditation all day long. Your command makes me wiser than my enemies, for it is always with me. I have more insight than all my teachers because Your decrees are my meditation. I understand more than the elders because I obey Your precepts. I have kept my feet from every evil path to follow Your word. I have not turned from Your judgments, for You Yourself have instructed me. How sweet Your word is to my taste—sweeter than honey in my mouth. I gain understanding from Your precepts; therefore I hate every false way. (Ps. 119:97–104)

Song 14: Your Decrees as a Heritage

Your word is a lamp for my feet and a light on my path. I have solemnly sworn to keep Your righteous judgments. I am severely afflicted; LORD, give me life through Your word. LORD, please accept my willing offerings of praise, and teach me Your judgments. My life is constantly in danger, yet I do not forget Your instruction. The wicked have set a trap for me, but I have not wandered from Your precepts. I have Your decrees as a heritage forever; indeed, they are the joy of my heart. I am resolved to obey Your statutes to the very end. (Ps. 119:105–112)

Song 15: Sustain Me

I hate the double-minded, but I love Your instruction. You are my shelter and my shield; I put my hope in Your word. Depart from me, you evil ones, so that I may obey my God's commands. Sustain me as You promised, and I will live; do not let me be ashamed of my hope. Sustain me so that I can be safe and be concerned with Your statutes continually. You reject all who stray from Your statutes, for their deceit is a lie. You remove all the wicked on earth as if they were dross; therefore, I love Your decrees. I tremble in awe of You; I fear Your judgments. (Ps. 119:113–120)

Song 16: My Eyes Grow Weary

I have done what is just and right; do not leave me to my oppressors. Guarantee Your servant's well-being; do not let the arrogant oppress me. My eyes grow weary looking for Your salvation and for Your righteous promise. Deal with Your servant based on Your faithful love; teach me Your statutes. I am Your servant; give me understanding so that I may know Your decrees. It is time for the LORD to act, for they have broken Your law. Since I love Your commands more than gold, even the purest gold, I carefully follow all Your precepts and hate every false way. (Ps. 119:121–128)

Song 17: I Pant for Your Word

Your decrees are wonderful; therefore I obey them. The revelation of Your words brings light and gives understanding to the inexperienced. I pant with open mouth because I long for Your commands. Turn to me and be gracious to me, as is Your practice toward those who love Your name. Make my steps steady through Your promise; don't let any sin dominate me. Redeem me from human oppression, and I will keep Your precepts. Show favor to Your servant, and teach me Your statutes. My eyes pour out streams of tears because people do not follow Your instruction. (Ps. 119:129–136)

Song 18: Everlasting Righteousness

You are righteous, LORD, and Your judgments are just. The decrees You issue are righteous and altogether trustworthy. My anger overwhelms me because my foes forget Your words. Your word is completely pure, and Your servant loves it. I am insignificant and despised, but I do not forget Your precepts. Your righteousness is an everlasting righteousness, and Your instruction is true. Trouble and distress have overtaken me, but Your commands are my delight. Your decrees are righteous forever. Give me understanding, and I will live. (Ps. 119:137–144)

Song 19: I Put My Hope in Your Word

I call with all my heart; answer me, LORD. I will obey Your statutes. I call to You; save me, and I will keep Your decrees. I rise before dawn and cry out for help; I put my hope in Your word. I am awake through each watch of the night to meditate on Your promise. In keeping with Your faithful love, hear my voice. LORD, give me life, in keeping with Your justice. Those who pursue evil plans come near; they are far from Your instruction. You are near, LORD, and all Your commands are true. Long ago I learned from Your decrees that You have established them forever. (Ps. 119:145–152)

Song 20: Consider How I Love Your Precepts

Consider my affliction and rescue me, for I have not forgotten Your instruction. Defend my cause, and redeem me; give me life, as You promised. Salvation is far from the wicked because they do not seek Your statutes. Your compassions are many, LORD; give me life, according to Your judgments. My persecutors and foes are many. I have not turned from Your decrees. I have seen the disloyal and feel disgust because they do not keep Your word. Consider how I love Your precepts; LORD, give me life, according to Your faithful love. The entirety of Your word is truth, and all Your righteous judgments endure forever. (Ps. 119:153–160)

Song 21: Abundant Peace

Princes have persecuted me without cause, but my heart fears only Your word. I rejoice over Your promise like one who finds vast treasure. I hate and abhor falsehood, but I love Your instruction. I praise You seven times a day for Your righteous judgments. Abundant peace belongs to those who love Your instruction; nothing makes them stumble. LORD, I hope for Your salvation and carry out Your commands. I obey Your decrees and love them greatly. I obey Your precepts and decrees, for all my ways are before You. (Ps. 119:161–168)

Song 22: My Lips Pour Out Praise

Let my cry reach You, LORD; give me understanding according to Your word. Let my plea reach You; rescue me according to Your promise. My lips pour out praise, for You teach me Your statutes. My tongue sings about Your promise, for all Your commandments are righteous. May Your hand be ready to help me, for I have chosen Your precepts. I long for Your salvation, LORD, and Your instruction is my delight. Let me live, and I will praise You; may Your judgments help me. I wander like a lost sheep; seek Your servant, for I do not forget Your commands. (Ps. 119:169–176)

Did you know that Psalm 119 has a soundtrack? It does—22 songs that will help God's Word stick in your mind. As you listen, you'll actually memorize all 176 verses in Psalm 119 effortlessly.

John Kramp wrote the 22 songs and top Nashville session vocalists and instrumentalists recorded them. All 22 songs in The Psalm 119 Experience Music album are available for purchase on iTunes. Plus, when you download the album, you'll get the 22 instrumental tracks for the songs for free—44 tracks in one album.

Find out more at www.psalm119experience.com

Would you like to have a personal guide for *your* Psalm 119 Experience? You can.

John Kramp hosts *The Psalm 119 Experience Podcast* that you can download for free. Each episode features devotional insights as well as portions of the songs from *The Psalm 119 Experience Music* album.

Go to www.psalm119experience.com. There you will get all you need to listen online or to download the podcast for free through iTunes.

THE

PSALM 119

EXPERIENCE

PODCAST

JOHN KRAMP